Anglo-German Foundation for the Study of Industrial Society

The Anglo-German Foundation for the Study of Industrial Society was established by an agreement between the British and German governments after a state visit to Britain by the late President Heinemann, and incorporated by Royal Charter in 1973. Funds were initially provided by the German government; since 1979 both governments have been contributing.

The Foundation aims to contribute to the knowledge and understanding of industrial society in the two countries and to promote contacts between them. It funds selected research projects and conferences in the industrial, economic and social policy areas designed to be of practical use to policy-makers.

Titles include:

Bernhard Blanke and Randall Smith (*editors*)
CITIES IN TRANSITION
New Challenges, New Responsibilities

John Bynner and Rainer K. Silbereisen (*editors*)
ADVERSITY AND CHALLENGE IN LIFE IN THE NEW GERMANY AND IN ENGLAND

Maurie J. Cohen (*editor*)
RISK IN THE MODERN AGE
Social Theory, Science and Environmental Decision-Making

Dagmar Ebster-Grosz and Derek Pugh (*editors*)
ANGLO–GERMAN BUSINESS COLLABORATION
Pitfalls and Potentials

Rainer Emig (*editor*)
STEREOTYPES IN CONTEMPORARY ANGLO–GERMAN RELATIONS

Karen Evans, Martina Behrens and Jens Kaluza
LEARNING AND WORK IN THE RISK SOCIETY
Lessons for the Labour Markets of Europe from Eastern Germany

Stephen F. Frowen and Jens Hölscher (*editors*)
THE GERMAN CURRENCY UNION OF 1990
A Critical Assessment

Stephen F. Frowen and Francis P. McHugh (*editors*)
FINANCIAL COMPETITION, RISK AND ACCOUNTABILITY
British and German Experiences

Jens Hölscher (*editor*)
50 YEARS OF THE GERMAN MARK
Essays in Honour of Stephen F. Frowen

Eva Kolinsky (*editor*)
SOCIAL TRANSFORMATION AND THE FAMILY IN POST-COMMUNIST GERMANY

Mairi Maclean and Jean-Marc Trouille (*editors*)
FRANCE, GERMANY AND BRITAIN
Partners in a Changing World

William J. V. Neill and Hanns-Uve Schwedler (*editors*)
URBAN PLANNING AND CULTURAL INCLUSION
Lessons from Belfast and Berlin

Laura J. Spence, André Habisch and René Schmidpeter (*editors*)
RESPONSIBILITY AND SOCIAL CAPITAL
The World of Small and Medium Sized Enterprises

Howard Williams, Colin Wight and Norbert Kapferer (*editors*)
POLITICAL THOUGHT AND GERMAN REUNIFICATION
The New German Ideology?

Rüdiger Wink (*editor*)
ACADEMIA–BUSINESS LINKS
European Policy Strategies and Lessons Learnt

Anglo-German Foundation
Series Standing Order ISBN 0–333–71459–8
(*outside North America only*)

You can receive future titles in this series as they are published by placing a standing order. Please contact your bookseller or, in case of difficulty, write to us at the address below with your name and address, the title of the series and the ISBN quoted above.

Customer Services Department, Macmillan Distribution Ltd, Houndmills, Basingstoke, Hampshire RG21 6XS, England

---

Responsibility and Social Capital

The World of Small and Medium Sized Enterprises

Edited by

Laura J. Spence
Brunel University
United Kingdom

André Habisch
Catholic University of Eichstätt–Ingolstadt
Germany

and

René Schmidpeter
Catholic University of Eichstätt–Ingolstadt
Germany

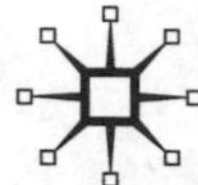

First published 2004 by
PALGRAVE MACMILLAN
Houndmills, Basingstoke, Hampshire RG21 6XS and
175 Fifth Avenue, New York, N.Y. 10010
Companies and representatives throughout the world

PALGRAVE MACMILLAN is the global academic imprint of the Palgrave Macmillan division of St. Martin's Press, LLC and of Palgrave Macmillan Ltd. Macmillan® is a registered trademark in the United States, United Kingdom and other countries. Palgrave is a registered trademark in the European Union and other countries.

ISBN 1–4039–4315–X

This book is printed on paper suitable for recycling and made from fully managed and sustained forest sources.

A catalogue record for this book is available from the British Library.

Library of Congress Cataloging-in-Publication Data
Responsibility and social capital : the world of small and medium sized enterprises / edited by Laura J. Spence, André Habisch, and René Schmidpeter.
p. cm.
Includes bibliographical references and index.
ISBN 1–4039–4315–X
1. Social responsibility of business. 2. Business networks. 3. Social responsibility of business—Germany. 4. Social responsibility of business—Great Britain. 5. Social responsibility of business—Netherlands. I. Spence, Laura J., 1968– II. Habisch, André. III. Schmidpeter, René.
HD60.R4725 2004
338.6′42′094—dc22 2004050116

10 9 8 7 6 5 4 3 2 1
13 12 11 10 09 08 07 06 05 04

Printed and bound in Great Britain by
Antony Rowe Ltd, Chippenham and Eastbourne

Contents

List of Tables and Figures

Tables

Figures

Acknowledgements

Our thanks to family and friends for their support during the writing and compilation of this book. The commitment of Brunel University, the Catholic University of Eichstätt–Ingolstadt and the Anglo-German Foundation to the research project on which this book is based was greatly appreciated. Much of the research in this book is only possible because of the generosity of small business people who, as we know, have many and varied calls on their time.

The authors and publishers are grateful to the following for permission to reproduce copyright material:

Chapter 3. L.J. Spence and R. Rutherfoord, 'Social Responsibility, Profit Maximisation and the Small Firm Owner-Manager, *Small Business and Enterprise Development*, Summer, 8(2), (2001), 126–39. With kind permission from Henry Stewart Publications.

Chapter 5. S. Janjuha-Jivraj, 'The Sustainability of Social Capital within Ethnic Networks', *Journal of Business Ethics*, 47(1), (2003), 31–43. With kind permission from Kluwer Academic Publishers.

Figures in Chapter 7. With kind permission from the Institüt für Mittlestandsforschung, Bonn.

Chapter 8. J. Graafland, B. van de Ven and N. Stoffele, 'Strategies and Instruments for Organising CSR by Small and Large Businesses in the Netherlands', *Journal of Business Ethics*, 47(1), (2003), 45–60. With kind permission from Kluwer Academic Publishers.

Notes on the Contributors

Keith Dickson is Head of the School of Business and Management at Brunel University and Professor of Strategic Technology Management. He has published and presented extensively on his research interests which centre on technological innovation in small firms, having successfully supervised European projects on research collaboration, scientific entrepreneurship, intellectual property rights, and telework.

Johan Graafland is Professor of Economics, Business and Ethics at Tilburg University in the Netherlands and Director of the Centre for Corporate Social Responsibility in the Philosophy Faculty. His recent publications focus on corporate social responsibility and the relationship with profitability and reputation.

André Habisch is Director of the Center for Corporate Citizenship, Catholic University of Eichstätt–Ingolstadt, Germany. In 2000 he was a member of the Inquiry Commission of the German Bundestag on the Future of Civic Engagement. Professor Habisch's research interests include social capital and corporate citizenship, on which he has published extensively.

Shaheena Janjuha-Jivraj is a Lecturer in the Business School at Brunel University, UK. Dr Janjuha-Jivraj's research interests include working relations, succession and family dynamics in small and medium sized enterprises, and the development of social capital among migrant communities during business start-ups.

Frank C. Maaß is Researcher at the Institute for SME Research in Bonn (IfM Bonn), Germany. He was a member of the expert group on 'Responsible Entrepreneurship for SMEs' undertaken by the European Commission in 2002/3. He works on business ethics, issues of new firm formation and strategic alliances among firms.

Lutz Preuss is Lecturer in European Business Policy at Royal Holloway College, University of London, UK. His research interests include issues in strategic management and European business and in particular 'softer' aspects of management, such as corporate social responsibility and business ethics.

Robert Rutherfoord is a Senior Research Officer in the Research and Development Division, Neighbourhood Renewal Unit, Office of the Deputy Prime Minister, UK. He previously worked for the Small Business Service, Department of Trade and Industry. When the work published in this book was written he was working for the Small Business Research Centre, Kingston University.

René Schmidpeter is General Manager of the Center for Corporate Citizenship, Catholic University of Eichstätt–Ingolstadt, Germany. He was educated in Germany and the UK. Mr Schmidpeter's research interests include social capital, family issues and corporate citizenship. He is currently completing his doctoral studies.

Clare Southwell is the CommunityMark and SME Development Manager at Business in the Community. She manages the national strategy for SMEs and the development of the SME standard 'CommunityMark'. Clare is a member of the National Small Business Consortium and the British Small Business Champions Award Steering Group and managed the European project on raising awareness of CSR.

Laura J. Spence is a Senior Lecturer at Brunel University UK and active member of Brunel Research in Enterprise, Sustainability and Ethics (BRESE). She was an executive member of the European Business Ethics Network (EBEN) from 1998 to 2002. Dr Spence has published widely on the ethics of small firms and comparative European business ethics. She is section editor for small business for the *Journal of Business Ethics*.

Nelleke C.G.M. Stoffele is a teacher and researcher at Tilburg University, the Netherlands, in the Faculty of Economics/Organisation and Strategy. She studied international business and graduated in 2002 in Corporate Social Responsibility.

Bert W. van de Ven studied economics and philosophy at Tilburg University where he now lectures in philosophical and business ethics, on which he has published in a variety of journals. Dr van de Ven's research interests are philosophical, business and advertising ethics, and the relationship between corporate social responsibility and competition.

Martina Wegner has conducted a comprehensive six-country survey for a German financial services provider to explore the possibilities of global sustainability strategies. She now works as a researcher at the Center for Corporate Citizenship (Catholic University of Eichstätt–Ingolstadt) and is completing her thesis on sustainable management from the perspective of multinational companies.

Andrea Werner is a PhD student at Brunel University, UK. Her thesis is on the contribution of Christian small and medium sized enterprise owner-managers to the common good in Western Europe. Prior to this she was at Brunel University as a researcher on the Social Capital, Civic Engagement and SMEs project funded by the Anglo-German Foundation.

List of Abbreviations

B2B	Business to Business
B2C	Business to Consumer
CC	Corporate Citizenship
CSR	Corporate Social Responsibility
DTI	Department of Trade and Industry (UK)
EC	European Commission
EU	European Union
ISO	International Standards Organisation
NGO	Non-Governmental Organisation
NIE	New Institutional Economics
SME	Small and Medium Sized Enterprise
UK	United Kingdom
US(A)	United States (of America)

Introduction

Laura J. Spence, Andrea Werner and Martina Wegner

While small and medium sized enterprises rarely attract national media attention and may not have significant effects on the economy taken individually, they constitute a significant proportion of the economy and society in Europe. However, there is a mismatch in the expectations of achievements of small and medium sized enterprises (SMEs) and the support and recognition given to them. Politicians look to SMEs as the engine of the economy, and as a key delivery mechanism for policy. SMEs consider that they are unfairly imposed upon by governments without a clear understanding of the reality of the world in which they operate. The latest in a long line of 'desirable activities' encouraged by government is corporate social responsibility. This is against a backdrop of very limited awareness of the existing social engagement of SMEs.

Since corporate social responsibility (CSR) research has largely neglected to consider SMEs, the contribution of this book is the drawing together of perspectives on small and medium sized enterprises and their engagement with social issues. Our approach encompasses a European dimension and, along with social responsibility, has a common theme of social capital in several chapters. This then is one of the first social responsibility and social capital texts with a small and medium sized enterprises, cross-cultural focus.

Social responsibility issues are on the political agendas of the countries under review in this book – Germany, the UK and the Netherlands – (Habisch *et al.*, 2004) and are increasingly related to SMEs. For example, in Germany the research commission of the German Bundestag into the future of civic engagement presented its report in 2002 (Commission of Inquiry of the German Parliament, 2002). In the UK, the Minister of State for E-commerce and Competitiveness, whose remit includes Corporate

Social Responsibility, is taking many initiatives forward as described in 'Business and Society: Corporate Social Responsibility Report' (Department of Trade and Industry, 2002). Engaging smaller organisations is one of the specific elements of the agenda proposed (ibid., pp. 31–2). In the Netherlands The Ministry for Economic Affairs funded a two-year research project (€1.4 m, 2003–2005) incorporating nine Dutch universities in a programme on corporate social responsibility (Cramer, 2002).

Our interest in SMEs should be seen against some statistical data. In the year 2002, 99.8 per cent of the UK's 3.8 million private businesses were SMEs (Department of Trade and Industry, 2003). The importance of SMEs is also reflected in Germany. In 2000, 99.6 per cent of Germany's 3,285,000 enterprises were classified as SMEs (Institut für Mittelstandsforschung, 2001). SMEs account for over 60 per cent of turnover and employment in both the UK and Germany (Lauder *et al.*, 1994) In the Netherlands, 99 per cent of private enterprises are SMEs representing more than 515,000 companies which employ 60 per cent of the Dutch labour force and account for 52 per cent of private sector income (MKB Nederland, 2003). The European Union definition of an SME is given in Appendix A.1, and is basically defined as having fewer than 250 employees. While there are weaknesses to this approach (Hauser, 2000; Curran and Blackburn, 2001, pp. 8–19), it at least offers a basic unit for ease of comparison.

Some may wonder whether it is necessary to consider SMEs separately from large firms; are they really so different? In fact, small firms are not just scaled down versions of their larger counterparts. The idiosyncrasies of small firms include that they are independent and owner-managed, stretched by a broad range of tasks, have limited cash flow and associated survival challenges, are built on personal relationships, are mistrustful of bureaucracy and are controlled by informal mechanisms (Spence, 1999). Perhaps the most significant perspective from the point of view of social responsibility is the role of the owner-manager of a small firm. The normal 'large firm' assumption focuses on managing directors with responsibilities to shareholders and the separation of ownership and control. In fact the most common business form is the small independent trader, who is both owner and controller of the firm as an owner-manager. Lack of separation of ownership and control allows the key organisational decision-maker to act as principal, not just agent. Hence the legitimacy of making personal decisions with company money, such as charitable donations, is considerable. A further critical difference for the small firm is the orientation towards profit. Small firms are not typically seeking profit-maximisation (see Goffee and Scase, 1995, and Chapter 3 in this volume).

Small and medium sized enterprises often play a particular role in civil society, for example as a local employer or investor, but also in the way they contribute to a community's social capital (Habisch *et al.*, 2001). Social capital refers to networks, norms and institutions that enable collective action among the individual players of society including authorities, companies, non-governmental organisations (NGOs) and interest groups. Social capital can be seen as an economically credible way of discussing issues of social responsibility and contributions made by business or other groups to society. As Portes notes, 'diverse sources of capital reduce[s] the distance between the sociological and economic perspectives' (1998, pp. 2–3). There is increasing evidence that social capital is critical for societies to prosper economically and for development to be sustainable.

This book was inspired by a workshop entitled 'Small and Medium Sized Enterprises (SMEs), Social Capital and Civic Engagement' that took place at Brunel University in 2002. Participants came from across Europe – Germany, the Netherlands, Slovakia, Switzerland, Italy and the United Kingdom (UK) – representing academia, NGOs, governmental institutions and practitioners. The workshop presentations led to very lively discussions incorporating the complexity of viewing social responsibility and social capital from differing interdisciplinary perspectives; economics, sociology, management studies and philosophy were embedded in the responses of the participants.

The workshop formed an integral part of a joint Anglo-German Foundation research project between the Center for Corporate Citizenship (CCC), Catholic University of Eichstätt–Ingolstadt in Bavaria, Germany, and Brunel Research in Enterprise, Sustainability and Ethics (BRESE), Brunel University, London, United Kingdom. The starting point of the project was the theory of social capital, which has received much attention from academics, NGOs and policy-makers as a possible solution to societal problems. The research objective was to gain an understanding of what role social capital, and in particular civic engagement as one manifestation of social capital, plays in the businesses and lives of SME owner-managers in a German–UK cross-country comparison, and to draw possible policy implications. Chapter 4 presents some key findings of the study.

The chapters in this book reflect the range of contributions made to the workshop, with some further perspectives stimulated by the event itself. In addition, Chapters 3, 5 and 8 are reprints of journal articles but speak directly to the themes of the book. We have been flexible in including debates referring to social responsibility, social capital, corporate citizenship and business ethics, offering varied perspectives on the broader issue of social engagement.

Since social capital plays an important role in the book, Chapter 1 constitutes a wide-ranging summary of the relevant literature, introducing the origins, types and character of social capital. Werner and Spence include discussion of sources of social capital as well as its functions, highlight its downsides and risks and also present the problems of measuring social capital. The chapter ends with a brief introduction to the link between social capital and civic engagement in particular.

After this overview of social capital, in Chapter 2 Habisch elaborates on SMEs as an embedded part of their local environment, with wide-spread socially responsible behaviour. Previous research by Putnam, Coleman, Fukuyama and Ostrom is particularly drawn upon. Social capital is proposed as a means to highlight the economic advantages of engagement and legitimise corporate social responsibility for small and medium sized enterprises. Benefits are seen with regard to improved reputation, risk-management, information gains and local knowledge.

The owner-manager of the SME is at the centre of Chapter 3 presenting an analysis of the social and ethical orientation of small firm owner-managers. Using a methodological approach by sociologist Erving Goffman it is proposed by Spence and Rutherfoord that there are four 'frames' for perceiving the social perspective of the small business. If policy-makers wish to influence the ethics of small firms they need to be aware of this diversity of viewpoints and move beyond the notion of the profit-maximising, rational economic entrepreneur as the standard image of the small business owner-manager.

In Chapter 4 Schmidpeter and Spence present the key findings of the comparative cross-national research in West London and Bavaria. The results relate to five relevant categories, which are formal engagement, networking within sectors, networking across sectors, volunteerism and giving to charity, and finally a focus on why people engage. It highlights the impact of sector differences compared with national differences and also outlines the restrictions to SME engagement.

Chapter 5 examines informal networks that support the British Asian business community. The chapter presents results from research on a network of businesses in Greater London. Janjuha-Jivraj discusses how ethnic communities have been important for facilitating the economic development of their migrant members, as they make the transition from economic refugees to citizens. However, there is a distinct difference in attitudes between first and second generations in terms of accepting business support from the ethnic community. This issue is further compounded by difficulties of external support agencies penetrating ethnic businesses.

Chapters 6, 7 and 8 present three larger-scale research projects on social engagement and SMEs. In Chapter 6, Southwell presents the British perspective in the form of a comprehensive study on SMEs and their engagement in social and community issues in the UK conducted by an intermediary, Business in the Community, on behalf of the Department of Trade and Industry. The chapter suggests that SMEs are widely engaged with social and environmental issues and that encouragement and support rather than formalised compulsory frameworks is the best way of promoting this further.

Frank Maaß of the Institut für Mittelstandsforschung (Research Institute for Small and Medium Sized Enterprises) in Bonn presents the findings of a quantitative research study on SMEs and corporate citizenship in Germany and interprets them from the new institutional economics perspective in Chapter 7. In a comparison with large firms, it is found that SMEs are actively engaged in corporate citizenship.

Chapter 8 by Graafland, van de Ven and Stoffele refers to a survey from the Netherlands analysing the use of strategies and instruments for organising corporate social responsibility. Results include statements on SME application of Codes of Conduct, International Standards Organisation (ISO) certification and social reporting. The study takes factors such as company size, organisational structure and sectors into consideration.

Most of the foregoing chapters present an overtly positive perspective on SME and their social engagement. This is balanced in part by Chapter 9 offering a critical view on the philosophical aspects of social capital. Preuss proposes an ethical test for social capital based on Aristotelian virtue ethics.

The concluding Chapter 10 by the Anglo-German Foundation project team presents future research issues and policy implications arising from this collection of papers.

We see this text as an example of the ongoing dialogue on SMEs and social engagement. The German–UK–Dutch discourse has proved fruitful and one which we foresee continuing. However, this can only serve as an example and underlines the necessity to bring in other national perspectives and research on our subject.

We hope that policy-makers, SME intermediaries and associations will benefit from the concrete perspectives on the social world of SMEs presented in this book and that it may inspire academic colleagues and students to do further research on these issues.

References

Commission of Inquiry of the German Parliament, *The Future of Civic Engagement*, (Enquete-Kommission des Deutschen Bundestages, *Zukunft des bürgergesellschaftlichen Engagements*) (Berlin: Deutscher Bundestag, 2002).

Cramer, J., Universiteiten starten onderzoek maatschappelijk verantwoord ondernemen (MVO), (www.eur.nl/fsw/esm/mvo, 2002), accessed September 1, 2003.

Curran, J. and R. Blackburn, *Researching the Small Enterprise* (London: Sage, 2001).

Department of Trade and Industry, *Business and Society: Corporate Social Responsibility Report 2002* (London: Department of Trade and Industry, 2002).

Department of Trade and Industry, *Small and Medium Sized Enterprises (SME) Statistics for the UK, 2002* (www.sbs.gov.uk/content/statistics, 2003), accessed March 14, 2004.

Goffee, R. and R. Scase, *Corporate Realities: The Dynamics of Large and Small Organizations* (London: International Thomson Business Press, 1995).

Habisch, A., J. Jonker, M.Wegner and R. Schmidpeter (eds), *Corporate Social Responsibility Across Europe–Discovering National Perspectives* (Berlin: Springer-Verlag, 2004)

Habisch, A., H.P. Meister and R. Schmidpeter (eds), *Corporate Citizenship as Investing in Social Capital* (Berlin: Logos-Verlag, 2001)

Hauser, H-E., *SMEs in Germany: Facts and Figures 2000* (Bonn: Institut für Mittelstandsforschung, 2000).

Institut für Mittelstandsforschung, *Mittelstand – Definition and Key Figures* (www.ifm-bonn.org/dienste/daten-engl.htm, 2001), accessed April 19, 2002.

Lauder, D., G. Boocock and J. Presley, 'The System of support for SMEs in the UK and Germany', *European Business Review*, 94(1), (1994) 9–16.

MKB Nederland, *MKB-Nederland* (www.mkb.nl/mkbnederland/english.shtml, 2003), accessed September 1, 2003.

Portes, A., 'Social Capital: Its Origins and Applications in Modern Sociology', *Annual Review of Sociology*, 24, (1998) 1–24.

Spence, L.J., 'Does Size Matter? The State of the Art in Small Business Ethics', *Business Ethics: A European Review*, 8(3), (1999) 163–74.

1

Literature Review: Social Capital and SMEs

Andrea Werner and Laura J. Spence

In this chapter, an overview is given of some key perspectives on social capital as drawn from the literature.[1] These include an introduction to the nature of social capital, its sources and effects and different types. The issues of measuring social capital are discussed, and the concept is put into the context of this book with particular foci on small and medium sized enterprises (SMEs), the wider society and civic engagement.

The concept of social capital has been paid much attention by a wide range of academics in recent years. It is characterised by contributions from a variety of disciplines, including political sciences, sociology, organisation theory and management studies. Key examples include the work of Elinor Ostrom (1990), a political scientist, who investigated how collective problems arising from the use of common pool resources can be solved through norms and institutions that pursue a middle way between third party enforcement and imposing privatisation. She looked at how irrigation institutions in Spain and in the Philippines have been organised. Another academic in the same field, Robert Putnam (1993), compared northern and southern Italy. His view is that through civic connectedness and engagement democracies become more effective and regions more prosperous economically. Sociologist James Coleman recognised the importance of social capital in the creation of human capital by looking at the drop-out rates of schools and their negative correlation to the support of parents and the religious community (Coleman, 1988). Similarly, Nahapiet and Ghoshal (1998), organisational theorists, have pointed out how social and intellectual capital within an organisation are mutually reinforcing and can lead to organisational advantage.

Network theorist Mark Granovetter (1973) emphasised the 'strength of weak ties' that help individuals, for example, to access information and jobs. He defines the strength of an interpersonal tie by the combination of the amount of time, the emotional intensity, the intimacy (mutual confiding) and the reciprocal services which characterise the tie (ibid., p. 1361). Finally, Burt (1992 and 1997), building on Granovetter's ideas, developed the concept of structural holes that actors can bridge and thereby benefit from, for instance in terms of career success. It is perhaps not surprising that the concept has also more recently been located in the management literature (Adler and Kwon, 2002).

The core idea of the social capital concept is that social networks (e.g. families, friends, acquaintances) have value (Putnam, 2000, p. 19). Social capital is engendered by the fabric of social relations and can be mobilised to facilitate action (Adler and Kwon, 2002, p. 17). Hence it can be described as an interactive concept (Habisch, 1999, p. 477). An important feature of the social capital concept is that of appropriability, i.e. the fact that social ties of one kind can often be used for different purposes (Adler and Kwon, 2002, p. 17). Woolcock argues that membership in distinct social groups is the context in which one gives and receives care, friendship, encouragement and moral support, but also provides (or prevents) access to key professional networks, political insiders and cultural elites (1998, p. 155). Another aspect of social capital is the principle of generalised reciprocity: 'I'll do this for you now, without expecting anything immediately in return and perhaps without even knowing you, confident that down the road you or someone else will return the favour' (Putnam, 2000, p. 134).

Although the ideas of social capital have been widely discussed in a variety of literatures (or perhaps in part because of the diverse approaches to it), the concept is, according to Adler and Kwon, 'still in the "emerging excitement" phase of the life cycle typical of an umbrella concept' (2002, p. 18). There remains some confusion in the literature as to how social capital is exactly to be defined. Adler and Kwon, for instance, mention the problem of whether trust can be equated with social capital, or whether it is a source or a form of social capital (ibid., p. 26). Because of this problem and also due to the vast amount of literature available on social capital (1,003 articles published between 1996 and March 1999, according to Putnam, 2000, p. 18), in the following we simply introduce some key themes or characteristics of social capital relevant to this book.

Origin, forms and character of social capital

Although aspects of social capital have been studied under different labels by classical sociologists such as Durkheim, Marx and Simmel (cf. Portes, 1998, pp. 7–9, and Woolcock, 1998, pp. 160–1) the term 'social capital' first came into use in the early twentieth century. Both Ostrom and Ahn (2001) and Putnam (2000) refer to Lyda Hanifan, a West Virginian state supervisor of rural schools, who coined the term having studied the roles of communities in satisfying individuals' social needs. For Hanifan, social capital refers to 'those tangible substances [that] count for most in the daily lives of people: namely good will, fellowship, sympathy, and social intercourse among the individuals and families who make up a social unit' (in Putnam, 2000, p. 19). Hanifan pointed out that building social capital not only improved the quality of life in the communities, but also trained students for 'meeting later in life situations of a public nature' (in Ostrom and Ahn, 2001).

As exemplified at the beginning of this chapter, social capital is not a unidimensional concept. Ostrom and Ahn identify three broad forms: (1) networks, (2) trust and norms of reciprocity, and (3) both formal and informal rules and institutions (ibid.).

The minimalist and often instrumental usage of social capital is most often found in social network analysis (ibid.). Here the emphasis is laid on the formal structure of ties that make up the social network, such as structural holes and closure (Adler and Kwon, 2002, p. 23). An example of the very narrow definition of social capital, i.e. an understanding of social capital as equivalent to the value of an individual's access to favourable personal networks (Ostrom and Ahn, 2001), is Burt's 'egocentric network analysis' (cf. Adler and Kwon, 2002, p. 19). For him, social capital is simply the contextual complement to human capital (Burt, 1997, p.339). In his theory a structural hole argument defines social capital in terms of the information and control advantages of being the broker in relations between people otherwise disconnected in social structure (ibid., p. 340). Coleman's argument that the closure of social networks foster the creation of human capital, takes a broader view. He emphasises the public good character of social capital, i.e. that individuals benefit from certain social structures regardless of whether they have contributed to the emergence and maintenance of these structures (1988, p. 116). In their study of business networks, Blundel and Smith mention four types of inter-organisational networks: industrial districts or clusters as spatial concentration, supply chain networks, entrepeneurial networks (coming closest to Burt's ego-centric networks since they use personal contacts to create new ventures) and innovation networks (2001, pp. i–ii).

Adler and Kwon point out that many scholars also focus on the content of social ties such as commonly shared norms and beliefs, and abilities (2002, p. 23). Fukuyama, for instance, regards social capital as informal

norms that promote cooperation between two or more individuals (2001, p. 7) and that are related to honesty, the keeping of commitments, reliable performance of duties, and reciprocity (ibid., p. 8) – what might be termed

'civic virtues'. He argues that coordination based on informal norms remains an important part of modern economies, and arguably increases in importance as the nature of economic activity becomes more complex and technologically sophisticated (ibid., p. 10). Ostrom emphasises that norms affect the way alternatives are perceived and weighed, and also that shared norms help to reduce the cost of monitoring and sanctioning activities to enable collective action (1990, pp. 35–6). The concept of trust plays a central role here. Fukuyama points out that the ability to form organisations depends on a prior sense of moral community, i.e. an

unwritten set of ethical rules or norms that serve as the basis of social trust (1995, p. 90).

Perhaps a strict separation between network-focused and content-focused views is neither possible nor desirable. So, for example, Putnam points out that social capital calls attention to the fact that civic virtue is most powerful when embedded in a dense network of reciprocal social relations (2000, p. 19), thus emphasising the importance of content *and* structure of networks. This argument can also work vice versa: economists suggest that continuous market interactions in a commercial society lead to the development of bourgeois social virtues like honesty, industriousness and prudence (Fukuyama, 2001, p. 16).

The phenomenon of civic engagement as an aspect of responsibility is particularly relevant in this book and falls into all categories of Ostrom's catalogue (see especially Chapter 4). First, if civic engagement is understood as active participation in public affairs (Putnam, 1993, p. 87), then it can take the shape of formal or informal institutions that help to enable collective action. If a wider view is taken, i.e. any (active) membership in voluntary organisations, associations or other kinds of networks is counted as civic engagement, or rather 'civic connectedness', then structural and also normative aspects come to the fore. Putnam, for instance, makes an interesting link between norms and civic engagement. According to him, honesty, civic engagement and social trust are mutually reinforcing (2000, p. 136). Putnam argues that 'people who trust their fellow citizens volunteer more often, contribute more to charity, participate more often in politics and community organizations' (ibid., p. 137).

Although the term 'social capital' was first invented by sociologists the question is whether social capital is also 'capital' in the economic sense

of the term, i.e. if it is something that can be invested in and will yield a future return. There is no consensus in the literature about whether social capital is a private or a public good. Putnam maintains that social capital has both an individual and a collective aspect. Connections that are formed by individuals, for example, first benefit their own interests. However, not all the costs and benefits of social connections accrue to the person making the contact; social capital can thus be simultaneously a private and a public good (2000, p. 20). Coleman, on the other hand, emphasises the public good character of social capital and argues that individuals will tend not to invest because of this (1988, pp. 116–18). In the following we concur with Fukuyama's view that social capital is a private good but pervaded by externalities (Fukuyama, 2001, p. 8).

Adler and Kwon list some commonalities with other forms of capital. Social capital is a long-term asset into which other resources can be invested, with the expectation of a future (albeit uncertain) flow of benefits. It is both 'appropriable' (i.e. can be used for different purposes) and 'convertible'. Moreover, social capital can either be a substitute for or can complement other resources. Finally, like physical and human capital, social capital needs maintenance (2002, p. 22).

There are, however, important differences between this and other forms of capital, particularly physical capital. Firstly, social capital does not wear out with use, but rather with disuse (Ostrom and Ahn, 2001). Furthermore, since social capital comes about through changes in the relations among persons that facilitate action (Coleman, 1988, p. 100), it cannot be traded easily, e.g. friendships and obligations do not readily pass from one person to another (Nahapiet and Ghoshal, 1998, p. 244). Coleman points out that a major use of the concept of social capital depends on its being a by-product of activities engaged in for other purposes and so there is little or no direct investment in social capital (1990, p. 312).

Another frequently mentioned difference is the fact that social capital is unlike other assets because investments in its development do not seem amenable to quantified measurement (for the focal actor) (Adler and Kwon, 2002, p. 22). Closely related to this point is the fact that social capital in general is not easy to observe and measure (Ostrom and Ahn, 2001). These differences clearly demonstrate the limitations of treating social capital as 'capital' in a narrow economic sense of the term.

Sources of social capital

A useful starting point is Portes's distinction between the more economic or instrumental view of norms of reciprocity on the one hand and a more sociological or 'consummatory' view of internalised norms on the

other (1998, p. 8). Portes sub-divides the first category into reciprocity exchanges and enforceable trust. Reciprocity exchanges refers to the accumulation of obligations and to norms that emerge through personalised networks of exchange (cf. ibid., p. 7; and Woolcock, 1998, p. 161). Coleman explains that by doing favours for other people, so-called 'credit-slips' with an expectation of future repayment will be created (1988, p. 102). Enforceable trust refers to the insertion of both actors in a common social structure. This means that, firstly, the 'donating' actor may be rewarded for his 'self-less' actions by the collective rather than by the 'receiving' actor, and, secondly, that continuous misbehaviour may lead to collective sanctions or even ostracism (cf. Portes, 1998, pp. 8–9; and Habisch, 1999, p. 19). In other words, a trustworthy social environment ensures that obligations will be repaid appropriately (Coleman, 1988, p. 102). One frequently cited example that falls into this category is the rotating credit associations of South East Asia (e.g. ibid., p. 103).

Internalised norms can also be sub-divided into value introjection and bounded solidarity. Value introjection refers to an obligation that people feel to behave in a certain manner (Portes, 1998, p. 7). These norms are transmitted from one generation to the next through a process of socialisation that involves much more non-rational habit than reason or rational choice, and evolves from tradition, culture, religion and other pre-modern sources (Fukuyama, 2001, p. 16; and 1995, pp. 90, 103). In this context Fukuyama criticises the poverty of contemporary economic discourse that neglects the role of culture (1995, p. 102)

Bounded solidarity, however, is not the result of norm introjection during childhood, but is an emergent product of a common fate. It emphasises identification with a certain community as a powerful motivational force (Portes, 1998, p. 8). Similarly, Fukuyama sees one source of social capital in the shared historical experience of a community. One of his examples is Germany, in which after the Second World War a consensual approach to management–labour relations was undertaken – in response to the recent past. This ultimately led to the creation of the highly praised 'social economy' (*Soziale Marktwirtschaft*) (2001, p. 17)

Effects or functions of social capital

In order to underline the potential importance of the social capital concept for developmental policy, some effects or functions of social capital will be looked at first from a focal actor's, particularly from a firm's, perspective and later from the viewpoint of a broader collective. The next section in this chapter outlines the 'dark' side of social capital, to which attention should also be paid.

The most obvious direct benefit for a focal actor is information. Adler and Kwon argue, for example, that social capital facilitates access to broader sources of information and improves information's quality, relevance and timeliness (2002, p. 29). Furthermore, the normally high cost of information acquisition can be reduced through social capital (Coleman, 1988, p. 104). In addition to this, Burt suggests that the flow of information can also work vice versa: through referrals a focal actor's interests are represented in a positive light, at the right time, and in the right places (1997, p. 340). Influence, control and power constitute, according to Adler and Kwon, a second kind of benefit of social capital. Such power benefits help the focal actors to get things done and achieve their goals (2002, p. 29). These aspects of social capital are discussed further in Chapter 2 of this book.

A third kind of benefit is a reduced need for formal controls and is closely related to a high degree of closure of the social network and strong social norms and beliefs within the network (Adler and Kwon, 2002, p. 29). Habisch calls this the insurance function of social capital (1999, p. 482), whereas Adler and Kwon label this kind of benefit 'solidarity'. Furthermore, Nahapiet and Ghoshal suggest that social capital can be seen as an aid to adaptive efficiency and to the creativity and learning it implies. They claim that it encourages cooperative behaviour, thereby facilitating the development of new forms of association and innovative organisation (1998, p. 245).

All these benefits for the focal actor can be summed up as the economic function of social capital: a reduction of the transaction costs associated with formal coordination mechanisms like contracts, hierarchies, bureaucratic rules and the like (Fukuyama, 2001, p. 10).

Putnam mentions another benefit that goes beyond a mere economic function: social capital operates through psychological and biological processes and so improves individuals' lives. He argues that there is evidence that people whose lives are rich in social capital cope better with traumas and fight illness more effectively (2000, p. 289). Similarly, Habisch points to the identity function of social capital. He suggests that strong relationships convey emotions, such as security, love, motivation, and cognition, i.e. normative orientation, status, a sense of belonging (1999, p. 486). Typical of this identity function is the fact that monetary payment can destroy the motivations of the participants. Rather, participants appreciate the non-pecuniary benefits that they experience within the context of social capital (ibid., p. 487).

Adler and Kwon suggest that each of the individual benefits they have listed can also produce positive externalities for the broader collective (2002, p. 29). For instance, brokering of information may rely on a reciprocal outflow and so benefits the entire network. Furthermore, the positive externalities associated with a collective actor's internal solidarity would include civic engagement at the societal level and organisational citizenship behaviour at the organisational level (ibid., p. 30). Putnam lists a few more collective benefits of social capital: it allows citizens to resolve collective problems more easily, it greases the wheels that allow communities to advance smoothly and widens people's awareness of the many ways in which their fates are linked (2000, p. 288). In short, he claims that civic connections help make people healthy, wealthy and wise (ibid., p. 287).

Downsides and risks of social capital

Beginning again with looking at the focal actor, the following risks can be identified. First, since building social capital is fairly time-consuming, it may not be cost efficient in certain situations. Second, the power benefits of social capital may, in some cases, trade off against its information benefits (Adler and Kwon, 2002, p. 30). Nahapiet and Ghoshal point out the problem of 'collective blindness', i.e. that strong norms and identification can limit a group's openness to information and to alternative ways of doing things (1998, p. 245). Portes mentions the problem of excess claims on group members that can prevent the success of individual business initiatives (1998, p. 16). This goes hand in hand with the reduction of the privacy and autonomy of individuals in a 'dense' community (ibid., pp. 16–17).

For the broader collective, downsides or negative externalities are more numerous still. Adler and Kwon argue that brokering for informational benefits by individuals or lower-level units may lead to a tragedy of the commons for the collective. They mention the example of how excessive brokering among Research and Development scientists can hamper innovation. They point to the negative externalities associated with a focal actor's search for the influence gains of social capital, and finally suggest that strong identification with the focal group may contribute to the fragmentation of the broader whole (Adler and Kwon, 2002, p. 31). In addition, Portes mentions the exclusion of those who are outside of the network and so barred from access to information (1998, p. 15). He also argues that group solidarity can result in a lowering of the morality of norms (ibid., p. 17).

In the light of the potentially harmful externalities of social capital it is therefore important to ask how the positive consequences of social capital (i.e. mutual support, cooperation, trust, institutional effectiveness) can be maximised and the negative manifestations (i.e. sectarianism, ethnocentrism, corruption) minimised (Putnam, 2000, p. 22). A frequently made distinction between bridging and bonding social capital may help in investigating this problem further.

Bonding and bridging social capital

A focus on internal ties within collectives emphasises 'bonding' forms of social capital, whereas a focus on external relations stresses what has been called 'bridging' forms of social capital (Adler and Kwon, 2002, p. 19). Although here a sharp distinction is being made between bonding and bridging capital, Putnam points out that in practice many groups bond along some social dimensions and bridge across others (2000, p. 23).

Bonding social capital focuses on collective actors' internal characteristics, those features that give the collective cohesiveness, such as ethnicity, age, religion, gender, and social class, and thereby facilitate the pursuit of collective goals (cf. ibid., p. 20). Bonding social capital is good for under-girding specific reciprocity, mobilising solidarity (Putnam, 2000, p. 22) and offering social support and identity (cf. Putnam and Goss, 2001, p. 29). However, according to Putnam, it may also bolster people's narrower selves and may create strong out-group antagonism (2000, p. 23).

Bridging social capital focuses primarily on social capital as a resource that is inherent in the social network, tying a focal actor to other actors that belong to different social groups. Hence this form is characterised by diversity (cf. Adler and Kwon, 2002, p. 19). Bridging social capital can generate broader identities and reciprocities. However, since it will be mainly used for linkage to external assets and for information diffusion (Putnam, 2000, pp. 22–3), it might also be exploited in a more instrumental way (cf. Adler and Kwon, 2002, p. 19). This raises a dilemma: Whereas bonding social capital is less instrumental, it is more likely to produce negative externalities. On the other hand, bridging social capital, which has the potential to produce positive externalities, is of a more instrumental nature. And so it might be a difficult task to optimise the positive effects of both social capital dimensions. Perhaps it is helpful in this context to look at Fukuyama's 'radius of trust' concept. He argues that if a group's social capital produces positive externalities, the radius of trust can be larger than the group itself (2001, p. 8). Fukuyama refers here to the historical example of the Puritans, who were enjoined to practise moral behaviour to all human beings and not just to kin and co-religionists (ibid., p. 14). He points out (with reference to Max Weber) that it was the moral values inculcated by Puritanism, and particularly the fact that virtues like honesty and reciprocity now had to be practised beyond the family, that made the modern capitalist world possible in the first place (ibid., p. 17). So Fukuyama's argument may imply that a virtuous approach could overcome the instrumental view of bridging social capital.

The problem of measuring social capital

Fukuyama claims that one of the greatest weaknesses of the social capital concept is the absence of consensus on how to measure it (2001, p. 12). Again, approaches that concentrate on the network aspect or the extent of 'civic connectedness', and approaches that focus more on the content of social ties, can be found in the literature.

A frequently cited example for the network approach is Putnam's measurement of voluntary organisations (e.g. Paldam, 2000, p. 642). With this instrument both the average size of the group and the number of groups within a given society are measured (Fukuyama, 2001, p. 13). On an individual level the number of organisations to which the person belongs and the intensity of the contact the individual has with the organisation is measured (Paldam, 2000, p. 637). However, voluntary organisations constitute only one particular network to join and this instrument does not take the formation of personal informal networks into account (Paldam, 2000, p. 642). Moreover, Knack and Keefer argue that group membership is not significant in economic growth or investment equations, since harmful effects of 'rent-seeking' groups offset any positive effects of voluntary organisations (cf. 1997, p. 1273). Network density can be measured by mapping people's networks and weighing them up against the strength and importance of the links (Paldam, 2000, p. 644). Although here, according to Paldam, a 'network payoff' for the focal actor could potentially be measured, i.e. the benefits (or amount of money) a person can draw on her network(s) if necessary (ibid., p. 641), a sum of all 'network payoffs' would be a poor reflection of the overall effect of networks on society. The same argument that Knack and Keefer made concerning voluntary organisations would apply: any positive effects for the broader collective could be offset by negative externalities of personal networks.

A popular way of measuring the content of human interaction is the measurement of trust, or more specifically 'generalised trust'. Generalised trust is defined as trust of people in general, whereas special trust is the trust of known people or trust in particular institutions (Paldam, 2000, p. 640). However, survey questions such as 'Would you say that most people can be trusted?' are vague, abstract and hard to interpret (Glaeser *et al.*, 2000, p. 812). Fukuyama argues that this question will not yield much precise information about the radius of trust among the respondents or their relative propensities to cooperate with family, co-ethnics, co-religionists, complete strangers and the like (2001, p. 15). For more precise measures, Glaeser *et al.* conducted experiments playing trust games and combined them with a survey (2000). Another rather vague attempt to measure trust in a more general way is the famous wallet-test: here 'n' wallets are 'forgotten' in public places and the test is how many will be handed back (Paldam, 2000, p. 644).

A further means of measuring the content of social ties is the measurement of norms of civic cooperation (Knack and Keefer, 1997, p. 1256). Here, respondents were asked whether, for example, it is justified or not to claim government benefits to which you are not entitled, to avoid paying the fare on public transport, or to cheat on taxes if you have the chance. Knack and Keefer's findings from their cross-country research indicate that trust and civic norms exhibit a strong relationship to growth (1997, p. 1260). Paldam points to the fact that trust and (ease of) cooperation are strongly related (2000, p. 635).

A more comprehensive attempt to measure social capital has been undertaken by Narayan and Cassidy (2001) in developing a Global Social Capital Survey (GSCS). They claim that their instrument also takes characteristics of associations into account (2001, p. 62). In the GSCS, group characteristics include the following elements: number of memberships, contribution of money, frequency of participation, participation in decision-making, membership heterogeneity and source of group funding. Other dimensions of social capital measured in the GSCS are generalised norms, togetherness, everyday sociability, neighbourhood connections, volunteerism and trust (ibid., p. 67).

Social capital and SMEs

Nahapiet and Ghoshal point out that firms – in contrast to neo-classical theory – provide many opportunities for sustained interaction, conversations and sociability – both by design and by accident (1998, p. 258). We can equate an SME with what Ostrom calls an 'appropriator of a smaller-scale common pool resource (CPR)' (1990, p. 183). Appropriators are those who draw resource units from a common pool (ibid., p. 30). An SME could, for example, draw employees from a community or information from a formal or informal network. They then could be characterised by the following behaviour: 'In such situations, individuals repeatedly communicate and interact with one another in a localised physical setting. When individuals have lived in such situations for a substantial time and have developed shared norms and patterns of reciprocity, they possess social capital with which they can build institutional arrangements for resolving CPR dilemmas' (ibid., pp. 183–4). Due to their size and scope of operation, it is particularly true for SMEs that they do not live in an atomised world but are embedded in networks, communities or other ongoing relationships (see Ostrom and Ahn, 2001). This might imply that SMEs and their relationships to their environment are shaped by various forms of social capital rather than by ad hoc short-term policies of dilemma solving.

An example of how small-scale corporations can cooperate successfully is given by Putnam in his cross-regional study of Italy (1993, pp. 160–1). He mentions 'a third Italy' – although small-scale, being technologically advanced and highly productive. Scholars term such areas 'industrial districts'. Among the distinguishing feature of these decentralised but integrated industrial districts is a seemingly contradictory combination of competition and cooperation. Firms compete vigorously for innovation in style and efficiency, while cooperating in administrative services, raw-materials purchasing, financing and research. These networks of small firms combine low vertical integration and high horizontal integration through extensive subcontracting of extra business to temporarily underemployed competitors. The result is a technologically advanced and highly flexible economic structure.

Putnam argues that norms of reciprocity and networks of civic engagement are essential for the success of industrial districts: networks facilitate flows of information about technological developments, the creditworthiness of would-be entrepreneurs, the reliability of individual workers and so on. Innovation depends on continual informal interaction in cafes, bars and on the street. Social norms that forestall opportunism are so deeply internalised that the issue of opportunism at the expense of community obligation is said to arise less often. To sum up, it is the mutual trust, social cooperation and well-developed sense of civic duty that is critical in the small-firm industrial districts.

Social capital and society

Ostrom points to two current policy descriptions that aim to overcome collective problems: introducing a coercive force outside the participants' individual psyches, i.e. public control, or imposing privatisation, i.e. private property rights (1990, pp. 8–12). Both solutions have severe problems and they also neglect the contribution of civic society and other institutional arrangements mediating the space between states and markets (Woolcock, 1998, p. 153) – a gap that the social capital concept could fill. However, it should be noted that scholars are not equally enthusiastic about the concept of social capital. Portes, for instance, argues that the set of processes encompassed by the concept are not new and have been studied under other labels in the past, and that there was little evidence for believing that social capital would provide a remedy for major social problems (1998, p. 21). By contrast, Ostrom and Ahn maintain that social capital should not be treated as a fad nor discarded simply as a new label for old ideas (2001).

Many scholars agree that the role of the state – as the traditional key enabler for collective action – should not be overlooked in the social capital debate. Paldam, for example, points out that the ease of building and upholding social capital depends upon the environment provided by the state and its institutions (2000, p. 633). Although scholars generally agree about the 'passive' role of the state, there is substantial disagreement about whether active state intervention or policies foster or rather destroy social capital. Conservatives, such as Fukuyama, claim that states can have a serious negative impact on social capital when they start to undertake activities that are better left to the private sector or to civil society (cf. Woolcock, 1998, p. 157, and Fukuyama, 2001, p. 18). Liberal social capital enthusiasts, however, regard state–society relations as positive-sum. For them, a broadly participative civil society provides citizens with the organisational skills and information they need to make informed decisions while simultaneously providing a forum in and through which suitable political leaders may be identified, nominated and elected (Woolcock, 1998, p. 157). In addition, Warner argues that government programmes are most effective in promoting community-level social capital when they view participants as producers, not clients, and develop a facilitative, participatory and horizontal structure (2001, p. 189).

A useful framework that could help optimise social capital on a societal level is Woolcock's two-dimensional model. It outlines social capital on a micro-level, i.e. among members of a community or society, and on a macro-level, i.e. focusing on the state, along both the 'embedded' and the 'autonomous' dimensions (1998, p. 165). Woolcock suggests that on the micro-level the initial benefits of intensive intra-community integration (i.e. embeddedness or bonding social capital) must give way over time to extensive extra-community linkages (i.e. autonomy or bridging social capital) and thereby create more social opportunity (ibid., p. 175). On the macro-level, state–society relations characterised by overlapping ties providing connectedness (i.e. embeddedness) and strong intra-corporate relations ensuring organisational integrity (i.e. autonomy) are needed for countries to be developmental (ibid., p. 178). However, Woolcock argues that the most pressing issues for development theory and policy emerge from the interaction between both realms (ibid., p. 179). The ultimate goal is therefore to achieve high levels of both the embedded and the autonomous dimensions in the micro as well as in the macro sphere, something that Woolcock calls 'beneficent autonomy' (ibid., p. 180).

But how exactly can social capital be generated? Even if Ostrom and Ahn's claim is true that social capital is hard to (directly) construct through external interventions (2001), states can at least indirectly foster the creation of social capital by efficiently providing necessary public goods, particularly property rights and public safety (Fukuyama, 2001, p. 18). This goes hand in hand with Ostrom and Ahn's claim that national, regional and local governmental institutions strongly affect the level and type of social capital available to individuals to pursue long-term efforts (2001).

Furthermore, if at the community level interactions as extensions of work, school or play do not naturally occur, fora for interaction can be intentionally created and designed to encourage development of social capital (Warner, 2001, p. 188). Pinkepank (2001) and Schmidpeter (2001), for instance, have demonstrated how social capital of a region can be fostered with the help of a governmental programme. An innovation forum called 'Innoregio' was introduced to help develop and realise common visions for the East German regions and innovation projects that led to economic, social and cultural development after reunification. The partners involved in Innoregio continue to use the structures created through innovation projects for on-going collaboration and mutual benefit. Blundel and Smith argue slightly differently. They claim that networks cannot necessarily be created by the government but they can be supported. Therefore, there should be a shift from support for individual firms to supporting existing business networks (2001, p. v).

Another opportunity to generate social capital is education. Fukuyama argues that educational institutions also pass on social capital in the form of social rules and norms (2001). Similarly, an understanding of enlightened self-interest, i.e. self-interest that is alive to the interest of others, could be conveyed through educational institutions, following Putnam's suggestion that citizens in the civic community are not required to be altruists but rather to pursue self-interest in the context of broader public needs (1993, p. 88).

From a network perspective the appropriability of voluntary organisations should be paid attention to. Coleman, for instance, argues that persons that are linked in more than one context can use these 'multiplex relations' if they need help, etc., and so benefit from their 'civic' engagement (1988, pp. 108–9). Fukuyama mentions religion and globalisation as two further sources of social capital that should be focused on. He argues that religion has historically been one of the most important sources of culture, and is likely to remain so in the future. With regard to globalisation, Fukuyama points out that despite its threats it also leaves new ideas, habits and practices in its wake, from accounting standards to NGO activities (2001, p. 19).

Particularly focusing on small firms and their business networks (including linkages to other small firms but also to large firms, individuals and other organisations), Blundel and Smith suggest some more policy implications to foster networks (2001, p. v). For example, as they found in their study that business networks tend to be sector-specific and vary in scale and characteristics, they warn against 'blanket' policies and the assumption that a successful network model can be replicated elsewhere (ibid., p. iii). Also, Blundel and Smith suggest that governments should seek to ensure ease of entry to and exit from business networks, since a dynamism in these networks would be crucial for knowledge enhancement and innovation. Another important suggestion they make is that governments should be aware that institutional arrangements (e.g. with public sector agencies) can be threatened by privatisation and commercialisation (ibid., p. v).

Civic engagement and social capital

This final section of the literature review tries to draw together several aspects of social capital concerning civic engagement that have already been addressed in the preceding sections. As mentioned before, civic engagement in itself can be a formal or informal institution that directly influences the quality of collective action (e.g. an active membership of a local chamber of commerce, engagement in a regional forum for socio-economic development or membership of a Parent–Teacher Association). If, however, we understand civic engagement as engagement in all kinds of voluntary organisations, such as choral societies, churches, sports clubs and the like, a direct benefit to society might not be immediately observable, apart from the fact that it enriches the participants' lives.

But the indirect benefits that evolve from the fact that, through these forms of civic engagement people become connected in a network, might be worth investigating. Putnam lists several mutual benefits that can arise from 'networks of civic engagement':

- They increase the potential costs to a defector in any individual transaction and so provide effective sanctions.
- They foster robust norms of reciprocity and trust.
- They facilitate communication and improve the flow of information about the trustworthiness of individuals.
- They embody past success at collaboration, which can serve as a culturally defined template for future collaboration. (cf. 1993, pp. 173–4)

The various effects and functions of social capital, such as the informational and the insurance function, also apply to networks of civic engagement. Following Coleman's idea that (dense) networks create trustworthy social environments, they also foster transparency of actions.

Furthermore, Putnam (1993) argues that participation in civic organisations inculcates skills of cooperation as well as a sense of shared responsibility for collective endeavours. Moreover, when individuals belong to 'cross-cutting' groups with diverse goals and members, their attitudes would tend to moderate as a result of group-interaction and cross-pressures. A dense network of secondary associations would therefore both embody and contribute to effective social collaboration (ibid., p. 90). An issue linked to this would be the extent to which the network is open to new and/or diverse members.

However, we must be careful not to regard civic engagement as *the* crucial variable in determining the well-being of a society. As Knack and Keefer point out, positive effects of group membership can be offset by effects of membership in 'rent-seeking' groups that can be detrimental to society (1997, p. 1273). Knack and Keefer refer here to the notion that horizontal associations can hurt growth because many of them act as special interest groups lobbying for preferential policies that impose disproportionate costs on society (1997, p. 1271). Again, the contents of these social ties and particularly their externalities would then play a role in determining the overall effect of voluntary organisations on society.

To sum up, social capital could in future prove a useful concept, to which policy-makers should pay attention. The strength of the concept lies in the fact that social capital does not only have the potential to solve collective action problems but it may also lead to win-win situations for the individual – social capital can thus be seen as a simultaneously public and private good (Putnam, 2000, p. 20). However, the difficulty in treating social capital as 'capital' in the economist sense has been pointed out, hence it can at best contribute qualitative aspects to the economic discussion (Habisch, 1999, p. 493). A win-win situation may also go beyond a mere financial and economic gain: as Putnam emphasised, social connectedness itself has intrinsic value and contributes more to human well-being than does affluence (2000, pp. 327, 333).

Moreover, concentration on fostering structural aspects of social capital has the danger of producing negative externalities that can be detrimental for the wider society. This 'dark side' of social capital should therefore be kept in mind and negative effects minimised. Also, the dangers of 'over-embeddedness' for individuals should be considered, and therefore it may be useful to aim at Woolcock's 'beneficent autonomy' as a balance of embeddedness and autonomy, rather than to encourage too close 'engagement' as building of social capital.

The limits of the role that governments can play in directly creating social capital have been outlined. However, the means of fostering social capital indirectly, by providing the conditions and environments that encourage social capital building, should be sought out. It remains to be seen whether social capital will be able to go beyond being a theory that points to the empirical facts of social connectedness and cooperation, and help solve societal problems as well as contribute to the fostering of human well-being.

Note

1. This chapter has benefitted greatly from discussions with André Habisch and René Schmidpeter. We thank them for their guidance on the social capital literature.

References

Adler, P. and S.-W. Kwon, 'Social Capital: Prospects for a New Concept', *Academy of Management Review*, 27(1), (2002) 17–40.

Blundel, R. and D. Smith, *Networking* (London: Small Business Service, 2001).

Burt, R., *Structural Holes* (Cambridge, Massachusetts: Harvard University Press, 1992).

Burt, R., 'The Contingent Value of Social Capital', *Administrative Science Quarterly*, 342, (1997) 339–65.

Coleman, J., 'Social Capital in the Creation of Human Capital', *American Journal of Sociology*, 94 (supplement), (1988) 95–120.

Coleman, J., *Foundations of Social Theory* (Cambridge, Massachusetts: Harvard University Press, 1990).

Fukuyama, F., 'Social Capital and the Global Economy', *Foreign Affairs*, 74(5), (1995) 89–103.

Fukuyama, F., 'Social Capital, Civil Society and Development', *Third World Quarterly*, 22(1), (2001) 7–20.

Glaeser, E., D. Laibson, J. Scheinkman, and C. Soutter, 'Measuring Trust', *The Quarterly Journal of Economics*, 115(3), (2000) 811–46.

Granovetter, M., 'The Strength of Weak Ties', *American Journal of Sociology*, 78(6), (1973) 1360–80.

Habisch, A., 'Sozialkapital', in W. Korff (ed.), *Handbuch der Wirtschaftsethik*, Band 4 (Gütersloh: Gütersloher Verlaghaus, 1999), pp. 472–509.

Habisch, A., H.P. Meister and R. Schmidpeter (eds), *Corporate Citizenship as Investing in Social Capital* (Berlin: Logos-Verlag, 2001).

Knack, S. and P. Keefer, 'Does Social Capital Have an Economic Payoff? A Cross-Country Investigation', *Quarterly Journal of Economics*, 112(4), (1997) 1251–88.

Nahapiet, J. and S. Ghoshal, 'Social Capital, Intellectual Capital, and the Organizational Advantage', *Academy of Management Review*, 23(2) (1998) 242–66.

Narayan, D. and M. Cassidy, 'A Dimensional Approach to Measuring Social Capital: Development and Validation of a Social Capital 'Inventory', *Current Sociology*, 49(2), (2001) 59–102.

Ostrom, E., *Governing the Commons: The Evolution of Institutions for Collective Action* (New York: Cambridge University Press, 1990).

Ostrom, E. and T. Ahn, 'A Social Capital Perspective on Social Capital: Social Capital and Collective Action', Gutachten für die Enquete-Kommission, '*Zukunft des Bürgerschaftlichen Engagements*', Kdrs. Nr. 14/107, (Berlin, 2001).

Paldam, M., 'Social Capital: Definition and Measurement', *Journal of Economic Surveys*, 14(5), (2000) 629–51.

Pinkepank, T., '"Citizen Can" – Building Shareholder-Value as a Corporate Citizen. Examples from Germany showing how investing in Social Capital leads to win-win Situations', in A. Habisch, H.-P. Meister and R. Schmidpeter (eds), *Corporate Citizenship as Investing in Social Capital* (Berlin: Logos-Verlag, 2001) pp. 114–21.

Portes, A., 'Social Capital: Its Origins and Applications in Modern Sociology', *Annual Review of Sociology*, 24, (1998) 1–24.

Putnam, R., *Making Democracy Work: Civic Traditions in Modern Italy* (Princeton: Princeton University Press, 1993).

Putnam, R., *Bowling Alone: The Collapse and Revival of American Community* (New York: Simon & Schuster, 2000).

Putnam, R. and K. Goss, 'Einleitung', in R. Putman (ed.), *Gesellschaft und Gemeinsinn – Sozialkapital im internationalen Vergleich* (Gütersloh: Verlag Bertelsmann Stiftung, 2001) pp. 15–43.

Schmidpeter, R., 'InnoRegio Networks as Social Capital of the Region', in A. Habisch, H.P. Meister and R. Schmidpeter (eds), *Corporate Citizenship as Investing in Social Capital* (Berlin: Logos-Verlag, 2001) pp. 122–7.

Warner, M., 'Building Social Capital: The Role of Local Government', *Journal of Socio-Economics*, 30, (2001) 187–92.

Woolcock, M., 'Social Capital and Economic Development: Toward a Theoretical Synthesis and Policy Framework', *Theory and Society*, 27, (1998)151–208.

2 Social Responsibility, Social Capital and SMEs

André Habisch

In this chapter, the detail of social capital theory as it applies to social responsibility is expanded and put into a European and a global context.

It could be argued that small and medium sized enterprises feel and act as members of their local communities more than large organisations. They have sometimes been present in their region for many decades. Owners, with their families, often live in the local area and have an interest in the resolution of local problems. Therefore SMEs – the German 'Mittelstand' – could be said always to have been a backbone of 'Corporate Social Responsibility' (CSR) or of 'Corporate Citizenship' (CC) in their communities. However, research and publications so far in these areas have not taken much notice of their engagement. Rather, important publications and collections of 'best practice' have focused predominantly on the activities of large companies. Many reasons for this include the following.

First, the most important fact is that there is still limited systematic academic research on CSR or CC at universities or research centres. This might hold true even more for Germany and Continental Europe than it does for the United Kingdom (UK). In the UK, active research is established at a number of research centres including Brunel Research in Enterprise, Sustainability and Ethics (BRESE), the International Centre for Corporate Social Responsibility (ICCSR) at Nottingham University, Business Relationships, Accountability, Sustainability and Society (BRASS) at Cardiff University and Ashridge Management Centre. However, even in the UK, CSR does not form part of the regular academic career of a business student nor is it a fixed element of standard business practice. The existing publications and media have predominantly been edited by business networks or related institutions. These owe their existence to the money of large corporations and focus more on their activities.

A second consequence of the notorious lack of academic research in the area is the dominance of consultancy-related activities within the CSR field, again perhaps most relevantly in Germany. Even those doing more scholarly based research focus more on large companies which could attract interest from clients.

Finally, SMEs themselves do not tend to reflect on their own social practice. Many protagonists are motivated by moral or religious convictions but have no inclination to speak about their deeds in public. Others fear to expose themselves too much on social issues. They do not want to lose perceived credibility by giving the impression that they are more concerned about charity than the quality and competitiveness of their products. Some want to avoid being approached by further demands for financial or logistic assistance. Furthermore, the term 'Corporate Social Responsibility' could be construed as being irrelevant for small organisations since many of them are not incorporated, and hence not 'corporate'.

However, socially responsible practice within small and medium sized enterprises is widespread, bringing the advantages of gaining contacts and building 'tacit knowledge'. When a business is sold or passed on to the next generation this tacit knowledge and way of doing business may be lost because experiential knowledge is so difficult to share. The extent of this in Asian small businesses in the UK is discussed in detail in Chapter 5.

More research about motivations and advantages of socially responsible engagement is urgently needed. When traditional ethical or religious motivations are increasingly absent, rational reconstructions are needed in order to legitimise these practices. In this volume, such an approach is developed from the emerging empirical evidence on the social role of 'Social Capital'.

The social science debate on a national as well as on the European level is more and more conscious of the crucial role of civic engagement for the economic and political success of a region. As Robert Putnam (1993a,b; 2000) and others have shown, areas with a deep-seated tradition of mutual help as well as networks of cooperation form an important factor of sustainable economic and administrative success. Small and medium sized enterprises play a crucial role. In many ways they form part of citizen coalitions: cross-sectional networks of cooperation between business and schools, business and social work, business and cultural institutions, in order to overcome common problems in society. Widespread cooperative practices of citizens to confront pressing problems may be conceptualised as 'investments in social capital'. What is the meaning of this notion?

Social capital theory – a social science concept

Some years ago sociologists and political scientists opened up the discussion about 'social capital', which may offer a better understanding of the role of corporate social responsibility for modern societies. University of Chicago sociologist James Coleman (1988) interpreted the results of a huge empirical study comparing the educational attainments of private and public schools in the United States (US). Coleman attributed his findings – the overwhelming superiority of private and more specifically Catholic schools – to the fact that the latter are embedded in the structure of a parish community. Within such a social framework norms and values can be taught and reinforced throughout the whole lifespan of pupils. They gain a greater 'trustworthiness' than their contemporaries.

In Coleman's studies, the most important mechanism of linking schools and families was voluntary engagement of parents – and more specifically of mothers. The network, which is created by those volunteers around ordinary school life – preparing special events, organising days off, enriching classes – contributes significantly to the success of religious schools. It plays a crucial role for the educational attainment of the schools. Therefore, Coleman conceptualises these networks as 'social capital'. Where does the capital-character of this mechanism lie? 'Like other forms of capital, social capital is productive, making possible the achievement of certain ends that would not be attainable in its absence. For example, a group whose members manifest trustworthiness and place extensive trust in one another will be able to accomplish much more than a comparable group lacking that trustworthiness and trust' (Coleman, 1990, p. 555).

With Coleman introducing the concept, it took the seminal work of Robert Putnam to illustrate how social capital can benefit the economic and political performance of a society. Putnam (1993a) compared the performance of regional self-administrative bodies in northern and southern provinces of Italy. In the 1970s a constitutional reform had decentralised power from Rome to newly formed regional governments. Twenty years later, in northern Italy subjective and objective assessments of regional governments were much better than in the south. Even though the formal rules had been the same in all parts of the country, outcomes were different. A higher economic performance turned out to be a consequence rather than a cause of these asymmetries. However, Putnam points to some deep-seated cultural differences, which could be expressed as a lack of civil engagement and voluntary associations in the south. Referring to Alexis de Tocqueville's (1840) seminal book on the American democracy, he discovered a strong empirical correlation

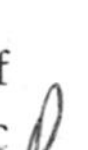

between the density of informal networks and voluntary engagement on the one hand and the political-economic success of a region on the other.

These findings fit into the broader discussion of the importance of 'trust'-relationships for socioeconomic development. Frances Fukuyama (1995) states in his popular book on trust, that cultural trust-bonds are a kind of social capital shaping economic and political performance of a society. In a low-trust culture, the lack of intermediary institutions and the notorious distrust between classes form a major obstacle for reforms in facing the challenges of economic globalisation. If trust is crucial for economic performance, this throws new light on the importance of 'non-economic' resources of a society:

> This trust is not the consequence of rational calculation; it arises from sources like religion or ethical habit that have nothing to do with modernity. The most successful forms of modernity, in other words, are not completely modern; that is, they are not based on the universal proliferation of liberal economic and political principles throughout the society. (Fukuyama, 1995, p. 352)

However, further deepening Fukuyama's argument it would be most interesting to ask whether a lack of 'traditional' networks and trust-potentials in society could be overcome by cross-sectional networks of cooperation between business and social partners. This is exactly the question development theory poses (Woolcock and Narayan, 2000). Social capital theory has proved to be especially fruitful for the reorientation

of developmental aid. The Social Capital Initiative of the World Bank (1998) offers broad evidence that structures of social capital are crucial factors for the success of development programmes and connects social

capital theory with the idea of self-reliance and institutional competence of a society.

On a micro-level the American political scientist Elinor Ostrom (1994) points out that local institutions, cultural norms, and rules of mutual control form an important asset in order to assure cooperation in developing countries. Therefore, Ostrom locates the concept of social capital precisely in the social science literature on 'collective action'. Problems of organising collective action in order to realise 'win-win-potentials' are omnipresent in human cooperation. As seventeenth-century Scottish moral philosopher David Hume puts it:

> Your corn is ripe to-day; mine will be so to-morrow. 'Tis profitable for us both, that I shou'd labour with you to-day, and that you shou'd

> aid me tomorrow. I have no kindness for you, and know you have as little for me. I will not, therefore, take any pains upon your account; and should I labour with you upon my own account, in expectation of a return, I know I shou'd be disappointed, and that I shou'd in vain depend upon your gratitude. Here then I leave you to labour alone; You treat me in the same manner. The seasons change; and both of us lose our harvests for want of mutual confidence and security. (cited in Putnam, 1993a, p. 163)

Mutual gains of cooperation between the peasants could not be realised, because even the fear of being exploited prevents every attempt to do so. Social science and modern game theory call that situation a 'prisoner's dilemma'. The lack of instruments to enforce mutual contributions remains a powerful obstacle against cooperation even if there are large potential gains for working together.

Putnam and Fukuyama see social capital as a decisive factor that shapes the business culture of an economy. Cultures of deep distrust make it very difficult to come together in order to finance public goods or to change rules for facilitating social and economic cooperation. But it also affects the nature of private companies. As Fukuyama states, in countries with a culture of trust and dense networks of mutual cooperation it was possible to form large stakeholder-owned companies, while in low-trust cultures, family firms with limited growth potentials prevail. From this perspective, social capital assuring means of cooperation and minimal consent is indispensable for the success of business enterprises as well as society as a whole – in developing as well as developed economies. It should be noted, however, that Fukuyama's analysis is a little superficial, since all cultures have small firms, most of which are not necessarily motivated by profit maximisation and growth (see Chapter 3).

Networks of cross-sectional cooperation may serve as social capital of a region if they enable their participants to create common rules, monitor their adherence and effectively punish (even on an informal basis) defectors. Thus, business enterprises working together as corporate citizens with partners from educational, social or cultural institutions are enabled to overcome dilemmas of cooperation and provide for public goods within such structures of regional social capital.

Investment in social capital as a business strategy for SMEs

Identifying social capital as a crucial factor for a region does not explain why business enterprises should invest in it. A theory that takes collective advantage as a sufficient reason for individual investment ignores the cooperation dilemma described above. This dilemma is even more vigorous for a small or medium sized enterprise. A citizen who agrees that certain activities are useful for regional society as a whole, might nevertheless reject the possibility of being involved in their provision. It is the prisoner's dilemma that prevails here. To ignore this simple fact results in a functionalist fallacy.

To explain the rationality of individual investment one has to mention the multiple effects of social capital for the different functions of the firm. Aspects that especially ally to SMEs will be mentioned here. They include:

(a) the building of reputation,
(b) risk management,
(c) gathering information and 'local knowledge'.

In the well-developed consumer markets of Western economies many 'homogenous goods' are offered. Whether you buy one kind of petrol or another, whether you book your flight ticket with this travel agency or another, whether you buy this car or another: there are no major qualitative or price differences left between competing offers. In this situation of many established options, reputation becomes a crucial factor for the 'product differentiation' of a producer or service provider. Adding 'social value' to the product – e.g. by engaging in the resolution of social, ecological or societal problems – 'makes a difference' in the eyes of many consumers, who prefer to buy a product which makes them feel good as a citizen. This effect may be deepened if the firm is collaborating with non-governmental organisations (NGOs). It is not only the credibility of socially responsible engagement that grows within such an alliance. The business may make use of the special knowledge of the NGO in order to confront the problem efficiently. Moreover, the connections of the NGO may serve as an 'information channel', spreading the information and introducing the enterprise as a responsible player who should be given preference over its competitors.

The management of risk is not often reflected upon but nevertheless forms a crucial aspect of investment strategies for social capital. Risk may be qualified in two dimensions. There are some completely exogenous business risks like weather conditions, earthquakes or (more obvious since September 11, 2001) terrorism. However, most business risks have at least some element of social interaction, in which the probability and/or the value of potential damage is influenced by behaviour towards the stakeholders. For example, even with optimal security mechanisms in place, the chemical industry might face an accident, one that sets free some dangerous substances or affects the larger natural and societal environment of the business enterprise. How sharp the reaction of the community, the employees and the unions will be heavily depends on the relationship that has been built up in the past. A company that has proven to be a 'good corporate citizen', investing in social capital for a long time, will be confronted in a very different way from that in which a misanthropic opportunist is confronted. Building networks of social capital and trust most obviously reduces the risk not of an accident itself but of the consequences a company might face (see also Waddock, 2001, on how companies build social capital).

Another important aspect of citizenship projects is the gathering of information. Information is a critical expedient for successful business in the twenty-first century. In an ever more complex society information does not only take the form of professional knowledge which could be bought from specialists or consultants. Local knowledge and information about important stakeholder groups is at least as important. This kind of knowledge can only be gained by interacting with these people and coming to know them personally. Important elements are the special needs and interests of clients and buyers. In Research and Development departments engineers run the risk of coming up with innovations which are only appealing to themselves and not to their ultimate constituency: the clients of the business. Therefore, some companies run corporate citizenship programmes integrating special groups such as school students and teachers, and handicapped and elderly people in the research and development process itself. The mutual exchange of information is an important utility that an active corporate citizen gains with engagement. Even for an individual, networks of social capital are an important source of information. For the company, engagement can become a device of collective learning and adapting to a rapidly changing societal environment. This aspect in many respects is even more important for an SME than it is for large international companies. They lack the resources to provide for professional information and market research agencies and are reliant more on 'informal' sources of information.

Institutional framework and mediating institutions: the European policy on CSR

In addition to traditional engagement in sponsorship and financial support, increasing numbers of SMEs engage in more permanent partnerships with social, educational or cultural institutions in their regions. The return of such stable cooperation may be very beneficial in terms of exchanges of mutual learning and specialisation. However, finding the 'right' partner could be as difficult as in marriage. Expectations from a partnership should correspond to each other and the value basis should at least be mutually compatible. Therefore, the task of arranging for such a partnership is a qualified activity. A culture of corporate citizenship is much more widespread where mediating institutions evolve and arrange for cross-sectoral partnership on a systematic basis. In many cities of the US for example, the 'Cares' organisations ('Chicago Cares', 'Greater DC Cares') provide such mediating services. Other elements of an institutional framework may contribute to lower the 'transaction costs' of an engagement for a firm. This includes elements of tax laws (tax deductibility of corporate citizenship expenses), the existence of local platforms for mutual exchange, attention of the (local) media towards corporate citizenship activities, information from the local Chamber of Commerce, and so on.

Among international institutions the discussion on CSR and CC has become very intensive. Recently the European Union (EU) Commission edited a note on corporate social responsibility of business enterprises. This summarises the results of a discussion process, which was started in the Green Paper of the European Commission (2001) entitled *A European Framework for Corporate Social Responsibility*. It fixes far-reaching commitments of European policy. The Commission wants to contribute to the emergence of a CSR culture in the European business context. In particular the commission intends to integrate the issue in the following realms of European policy: Employment and social policies; Enterprises; Environmental policy; Consumer policy; Public provision; Foreign policy; Development policy; Trade policy.

Reflecting the scepticisms of many stakeholders, especially in the business world, the paper affirms that the principle of volunteerism should be obligatory for CSR practices. The key commitments are:

1. To deepen knowledge about the positive effects of CSR on business and society in Europe and in the global context, especially in the developing countries.
2. To stimulate the exchange of experiences between businesses.
3. To enhance the development of CSR management competences.
4. *To stimulate CSR practices among SMEs.*
5. To guarantee the convergence and transparency of CSR practices and instruments.

6. To install a 'European Multi-stakeholder-Forum'.
7. To integrate CSR in EU policy.

Policies addressing SMEs are a special focus of the Green Paper. The Commission acknowledges that there already exists a widespread praxis of CSR among SMEs. The recent report of the European Observatory for SMEs on CSR practices – cited by the Commission's paper – formulates: 'Many SMEs already practice social and ecological responsible management even if they are not familiar with the CSR concept or regularly communicate about their practices. For many SMEs such practices are simply a consequence of responsible entrepreneurship' (Observatory of European SMEs, 2002). However, what is lacking for the Observatory is integration into a business strategy. The motivation is mostly ethical and a desire to strengthen relationships to local communities and consumers. The report shows that for many SMEs a positive correlation exists between an orientation towards innovation, quality and growth on the one hand and the measure of CSR activities on the other. An important problem, however, remains the shortage of financial resources. The Commission invites business associations, networks of mutual assistance and Chambers of Commerce to better inform SMEs about changes and strategies of CSR, and to come up with instruments to help them better integrate CSR into their business strategy. The Commission itself plans:

(a) To stimulate research concerning the existing practice and the economic value of CSR for SMEs.
(b) To foster cooperation with associations and experts from the member states.
(c) To develop user-friendly instruments and toolkits for SMEs in order to lower their transaction costs of engagement.
(d) To facilitate cooperation between large enterprises and SMEs (mentoring systems, etc.).
(e) To create public sensibility for CSR and stimulate the development of an institutional infrastructure in that field.

The paper of the EU Commission shows the lively interest of European policy in widespread socially responsible practice. Similar initiatives were put into practice by the 'Global Compact' Initiative of United Nations General Secretary Kofi Annan. In January 2000 Annan launched the Compact at the World Economic Forum at Davos in order to strengthen the cooperation between SMEs and large companies, national governments and civil society. Business should realise its responsibility in order to overcome pressing problems of the twenty-first century such as poverty in lesser developed countries, violation of human rights and the global environment. The 'Global Compact' is still *in statu nascendi*, but it is already helping to develop growing activities internationally.

More than 90 per cent of corporations are SMEs. If their social responsibility activities are to be strengthened, a 'culture of corporate citizenship' has to be developed. That implies growing awareness about their strategic advantages by management, but at the same time also a stimulating and cooperative social context. Further empirical research to better understand motivations and strategies is a crucial element here.

References

Coleman, J., *Foundations of Social Theory* (Cambridge, Massachusetts: Harvard University Press, 1990).

Coleman, J., 'Social Capital in the Creation of Human Capital', *American Journal of Sociology*, 94 (supplement), (1998) 95–120.

European Commission, *Green Paper on the Corporate Social Responsibility of Business*, Brussels, COM(2001) 366 final, 18.7.2001 (2001).

Fukuyama, F., *Trust: The Social Virtues and the Creation of Prosperity* (New York: Free Press, 1995).

Observatory of European SMEs, *European SMEs and Social and Environmental Responsibility*, 2002/No. 4 (European Commission: Enterprise Publications, 2002).

Ostrom, E., 'Constituting Social Capital and Collective Action', *Journal of Theoretical Politics*, 6 (1994) 527–62.

Putnam, R., *Making Democracy Work: Civic Traditions in Modern Italy* (Princeton: Princeton University Press, 1993a).

Putnam, R., 'The Prosperous Community: Social Capital and Public Life', *The American Prospect*, 13, (1993b) 35–42.

Putnam, R., *Bowling Alone: The Collapse and Revival of American Community* (New York: Simon & Schuster, 2000).

Tocqueville, A. de, *Democracy in America*, 2 volumes (New York: Alfred A. Knopf, 1840, 1935, 1945).

Waddock, S., 'How Companies Build Social Capital', *Reflections*: *The Society for Organizational Learning Journal*, 3(1), (2001) 18–24.

Woolcock, M. and D. Narayan, 'Social Capital: Implications for Development Theory, Research and Policy', *World Bank Research Observer*, 15(2), (2000) 225–49.

World Bank, 'The Local Level Institutions Study: Program Description and Prototype Questionnaires', *Local Level Institutions Working Paper No. 1*, May 1998, and *Working Paper No. 2*, August 1998 (Washington: World Bank, 1998).

3

Social Responsibility, Profit-Maximisation and the Small Firm Owner-Manager

Laura J. Spence and Robert Rutherfoord

This chapter[1] explores a relatively under-researched area: the role of ethics in small firms. It examines from the perspective of the owner-manager the types of motivations affecting decision-making and ethical frameworks within the small firm.

There are important reasons why ethics in small firms need to be examined more closely. 'Business ethics' sits across the intersection of the social, the political and the economic in the world of business. Milton Friedman's (1970) assertion that the social responsibility of business is only to increase profits is no longer sufficient in a world where governments are once again actively encouraging '*private*, free market, solutions to *public* problems' (Harvey, 1988, p. 131, emphasis in the original). The business landscape, despite the domination of major multinationals in certain sectors, continues healthily to be populated by firms of all types, sizes and sectors. Researchers are also now recognising the importance of business ethics as it applies to the small firm, instead of the previous research focus on large firms alone (Quinn, 1997; Vyakarnam *et al.*, 1997; Spence, 1999).

The attitudes and behaviours of the owner-managers of some 3.5 million small firms in the UK economy inevitably will influence to some extent their networks of suppliers, customers and employees. Indeed, 44.7 per cent of all private sector employees in the UK work for small firms (statistics in this paragraph are from Department of Trade and Industry, 1999). The economic impact of these organisations should also not be underestimated. In 1998 small firms accounted for 37 per cent of turnover. There is no location which is not dominated by small firms in numerical terms, since small and medium sized firms account for over 99 per cent of businesses in all regions (although regional sectoral density does vary across the regions). This is why, at least collectively, small firms and their practices play a significant role in the UK today, and should therefore not be excluded from debates on business ethics and social responsibility.

It might be assumed that an understanding of business ethics in large firms could be simply transferred to the situation of the small firm. Previous studies of small firms would, however, suggest that this is incorrect. Small enterprises are different in nature, not just in size, from large firms (Holliday, 1995, p. 2) and there are also important differences in the nature of business ethics in small firms. Particularly important is the fact that in the owner-managed small firm, control remains in the hands of one of the owners, potentially enabling him or her to make personal choices about the allocation of resources. In addition, the tendency for small firms to be dominated by personal relationships and the preferred, and often appropriate, absence of bureaucratic controls may enhance relationships of trust and openness in business relationships. Indeed, Goffee and Scase note that entrepreneurial enterprises, centrally controlled and managed through face-to-face contact, are able to 'be very adaptive, swiftly adjusting their trading capacities according to changing market opportunities' (Goffee and Scase, 1995, p. 18). However, the pressures on the owner-manager to deal with multiple tasks, the restrictions of cash flow (noted by Howorth and Wilson, 1999) and the need to deal with short-term problems may appear to result in a limited capacity to deal with those issues not directly affecting the survival of the firm. An example from research conducted in 1997 illustrates the reality of life for many small firm owner-managers. In a focus group, one noted:

> There is a balance of time on idea creation and then just being a straightforward managing director, to changing light bulbs – none of us small businesses have janitors. Or if a lady client is coming, checking that there is loo paper in the ladies loo. Literally it is as basic as that. Sometimes you go home and think 'what a waste of a day'. (Small Business Research Centre, 1997, p. 8)

These factors contrast with many assumptions about how large firms tend to be managed, strategically and with clearly delineated responsibilities and tasks.

This chapter reports on a research project which is intended further to open up the field of debate on ethics in small firms. It builds on an earlier review of studies on small firm ethics (Spence, 1999). This review found that no clear picture of ethics from the small firm perspective has yet emerged. Existing research has often tended to draw, inappropriately, on large firm management practices, such as evidence of codes, which are of limited relevance to the smaller enterprise (see, for example, Webley, 1997; and the focus on individuals in large firms in the *Business Ethics Quarterly* review of the past, present and future of business ethics [2000]). The review by Spence (1999) also proposed a research agenda clarifying the focus on small firm ethics by looking at the micro, meso and also macro levels. The study reported here is conducted at the micro level, i.e. on the owner-manager and his or her ethical perspective within the small firm. The conclusions drawn can hence only be accepted from the perspective of the owner-manager. This research does not incorporate direct evidence from other stakeholders.

Methodology: qualitative data collection and 'frame analysis'

A qualitative strategy of investigation based on semi-structured face-to-face interviews with small firm owner-managers was adopted in order to explore the factors influencing ethical orientation in the small firm at the micro level. Twenty small firm owner-managers in the UK were interviewed with a view to improving our understanding of the ethical issues which are seen as of particular relevance to the small firm *by the owner-managers*. In this study, we cannot assume that the other stakeholders of the firm are of the same opinion as the owner-managers. The qualitative methodology uses a semi-structured interview to explore the motivations, priorities and business practices of the owner-managers of the firms. The firms in the sample were in a broad range of business sectors, based in one county in the south of England. All firms were characterised by being independent, owner-managed and with fewer than 50 employees. Access was achieved by letters sent to 40 small firms in the area (randomly chosen from the business directory Kompass) and follow-up telephone calls to make appointments. A summary of the firms owned by the respondents is shown in Table 3.1.

As noted by Curran and Blackburn (1994, pp. 55–61), it was considered likely that there would be some business sector differences. The purpose of this study is exploratory, and a wide selection across the range of different sector types was desired in order to help identify any similarities in small firms across the sectors. Nevertheless, half of the sample is drawn from manufacturing sectors and half from service sectors in order to allow any preliminary sector differences to emerge.

The use of face-to-face interviews as the principal research tool was particularly appropriate in this study, as it was necessary to use a technique

Table 3.1 Summary of participating firms

Service/manufacturing code	*Main business activity*	*Year started trading*	*Number of employees*
Manufacturing BE1M	Wire products	1977	12
Service BE2S	Consulting	1994	4
Service BE3S	Product design	1991	2
Service BE4S	Mechanical servicing	1991	1
Service BE5S	Computer maintenance	1993	8
Manufacturing BE6M	Component engineering	1985	6
Service BE7S	Marketing	1984	9
Service BE8S	Antiques	1997	0
Service BE9S	Computer supplier	1984	38
Service BE10S	Computer maintenance	1997	8
Service BE11S	Architects	1996	5
Service BE12S	Translators	1986	0
Manufacturing BE13M	Furniture makers	1998	9
Manufacturing BE14M	Plastic moulds	1965	13
Manufacturing BE15M	Tape	1973	11
Manufacturing BE16M	Control panels	1972	19
Manufacturing BE17M	Bar code machines	1987	2
Manufacturing BE18M	Weighing equipment	1982	4
Manufacturing BE19M	Rubber gaskets	1957	12
Manufacturing BE20M	Interiors	1996	10

Note: Turnover data were not gathered due to sensitivity issues arising in the pilot study.

in which the owner-managers themselves can define, *in their own terms*, how their business is and should be run, and whether notions of 'ethics' fit into this. Liedtka (1992), for example, has considered in detail the use of interviews in empirical business ethics research. She notes that the primary benefit of using interviews is that they allow for deeper exploration of reasoning for actions within the social context than more generalisable, quantitative surveys, particularly if the questions are open-ended and the interviewer responds to the path the interviewee takes in answering questions.

Where the organisation was multi-owned and managed, the main decision-maker was interviewed where possible. The logic of focusing on the owner-manager is to access the potentially strongest influence within the firm. Whilst this occasionally may be a false assumption, the owner-manger is a consistent figure in the small firm and is often the person who established it. This is not to say that other members of the small firm are unimportant; they should be studied in other research as a focus of small business ethics. This research, however, focuses on the influence that the owner-manager has on the small firm as a key difference between small firms and large firms, and is therefore particularly interesting as an initial area of investigation for small business ethics.

One area of research interest was to understand whether business ethics – which we can consider to be the influence of social issues as well as purely commercial factors in decision-making – has a significant role in small business. It is important to note that the study was not presented to the participants as being about 'business ethics'. This was to avoid any preconceived interpretations and to help prevent 'socially desired responses' (Bain, 1993). The research was presented as being about priorities and practices for small business owners, which indeed it was. The face-to-face interviews allowed the contextualised discussion of how individual businesses are run with those responsible for the major decision-making within the firm.

Examples of key questions posed in order to allow some comparability between the responses were:

- Can you tell me a bit about your reasons for starting the business?
- What are your current priorities?
- How do you differentiate your firm from your competitors to win contracts (particularly other than price)?
- Could you describe your relationship with your business partners and colleagues (customers and suppliers)?
- Does your business make a contribution to the economy and society?

Under each of the questions was a list of prompts, which allowed the respondents to talk in some depth about these issues. By asking the respondents to talk around the key questions, a picture emerged of different ways of understanding the experience of running a small business in relation to the profit motive and social activity. Erving Goffman called different ways of understanding experience 'frames' (Goffman, 1974) and it was Goffman's approach, frame analysis, which inspired the analysis of the data. Using Goffman's methodology, from repeated reading of the transcribed material, four perspectives emerged which were identified from analysis of respondents' statements as ways of understanding their business life. The social versus profit-maximisation perspective gives an intriguing insight into the drives for running a business and how they cross ethical and social boundaries.

It should be pointed out that the use of Goffman's frame analysis is consistent with a clear orientation to an interpretation of ethics in terms of the actors. This work is clearly exploratory in nature, and this coupled with the ideographic position that we can only make sense of ethics in terms of the actors' understanding of their world, makes frame analysis an ideal choice. Objections to normative universalism in business ethics require a clear empirical understanding of the internal logic that actors apply to their actions (Enderle, 1996). It is intended that the research presented here goes some way to accessing the kinds of perspectives that those in the research sample hold on social orientation in their business organisations. No generalisations can be claimed, but it is hoped that the study may lead on to further investigation of social responsibility in small firms.

Goffman's work is a form of dramaturgical analysis which considers the roles played or carried out by the small firm owner-manager as socially located and categorised by the participants' understandings of 'what is going on'. Starting from the premise that while participants may not create them, definitions of situations can always be found, Goffman introduces the concept of frame analysis as an examination of the organisation of those definitions (or experiences) (Goffman, 1974, pp. 1–20). When talking about priorities and practices in the firm, the owner-manager responded to the interviewer by giving his or her understanding of the events, perspectives or interactions being discussed. Frame analysis can then be used to tease apart the 'layers, strands and meanings' of the elements of an interaction as experienced by its participants.

Erving Goffman (1974, p. 9) acknowledges that it is problematic to assume that any one perspective of an interaction is the unitary truth of a situation. However, it is the identification of these different perspectives that Goffman is interested in and terms 'frame analysis'. Hence, the four frames which are found in this data are four ways of viewing the relationship between profit-maximising and social issues in the small firm. Clearly, each firm would need to make a certain amount of profit in order to survive. However, in the interviews emphasis was placed on '*profit-maximisation*' rather than turnover or making *a* profit.

Each frame may be a perspective which is understood and experienced by any one owner-manager, or an owner-manager may consistently talk in terms which suggest the dominance of one single perspective, or frame, in his or her understanding of what is going on in the firm. Goffman himself acknowledges that he does not detail sufficiently the shifting from one frame to another, or how different frames can be openly and simultaneously sustained (Goffman, 1981, p. 67). However, this is a secondary level of analysis; the first stage is to satisfactorily identify frames which can be agreed upon in a variety of studies. The dynamics of those frames remains an area for future research.

The interviews were tape-recorded and transcribed. In this way the texts of the dialogue can be revisited, avoiding reliance on analysis based on first impressions made by the researcher. This technique also allows sections of dialogue to be presented to the reader in order to confirm or challenge the researcher's interpretation and subsequent data analysis. The data were analysed using manual coding to group the perspectives of the small firm owner-managers into frames of the small business experience (for a discussion, see Bryman and Burgess, 1994, pp. 195–215). The main results are presented in the remainder of this chapter.

In the research a distinction was made between the perspective of the owner-manager on the importance of profit-maximisation and the actions they reported. It was not usually possible to obtain any corroborative evidence of the actions reported. For example, they might say that they give regularly to charity, but it was not within the scope of this research to either prove or disprove such assertions. Nevertheless, the course of the discussions (up to one hour long) and the positioning of the research purpose as being to understand practices rather than be judgmental, on the surface at least enabled a non-threatening atmosphere and provided no real reason for being untruthful.

Avoidance of socially desirable responses was a key concern. Socially desirable response syndrome is where respondents reply in ways deemed to be socially acceptable. In business ethics research this generally refers to respondents answering questions with perceived 'morally correct' answers instead of genuine beliefs (Bain, 1993). Responses by some of those interviewed helped clarify this point. Paradoxically, in relation to the socially desired response syndrome, rather than imagining that the researcher wanted to hear about social and ethical behaviour some of the respondents implied that they felt they *should* be more profit-maximisation motivated. The socially desirable perspective in this case was to be profit-maximising, not altruistic. This may have been in response to the researcher's perceived role as someone coming from a business school where, it was assumed, profit-maximisation was analogous to successful business. An illustrative example of this is shown in the text below, where the owner of an antique shop comments how she 'should' be more financially ruthless:

> *Interviewer*: Do you take into account the circumstances of the person you are buying from?

> *Respondent*: Yes, unfortunately, *but you shouldn't.*
> *Interviewer*: How does that work?
> *Respondent*: Particularly if it is some old boy or some old girl that comes in . . . I find I end up offering them more because you feel so awful. *It is a case of ethics* and I think it is quite a difficult one to balance. I was saying to someone the other day it is between where's the line between making a reasonably good profit and getting to the point that you are cheating someone. Only you can make that decision. (italics added) (BE8S, Antiques Retailer, 0 employees)

Implied in this section of dialogue is that the respondent feels she should be more profit-maximisation orientated, but can't help being socially conscious and as a result is constraining her own profit. There is almost a sense of guilt evident, in talking to the researcher, that she is not more clearly profit focused. This was also reflected in other interviews. This type of exchange suggested that in fact the respondents thought that it would be preferable (desirable) if they could convey themselves as being profit-maximisers. This is in contrast to the assumption of socially desirable response syndrome that people will claim to be more *ethical* than they are. This is an important finding and not one that is associated with large firms, where the basic assumption is that they *are* profit oriented, and must be in order to satisfy shareholders, unless they defend themselves as being otherwise. Hence we have the unusual position of the owner-managers being relatively reluctant to admit to ethical and socially aware behaviour. Any bias in the data, in this respect, is most likely to be an *under*-emphasis on socially conscious, altruistic behaviour.

Results: the four ethical frames utilised by owner-managers

The data were analysed and four different ways of understanding the motivational experience of running your own business were identified from the interview transcripts. The frames were arrived at by repeated reading of the transcribed interviews and grouping of respondents' statements. The final typology resulted in four frames which fell into the framework shown in Figure 3.1. Consistent with Goffman's analysis it should be stressed that it is not necessarily the case that any one owner-manager will consistently adopt the same frame.

Represented on the two axes were factors which were discussed in the course of the interviews with the owner-managers. On the horizontal axis, the notion of profit-maximisation should be clarified. All of the

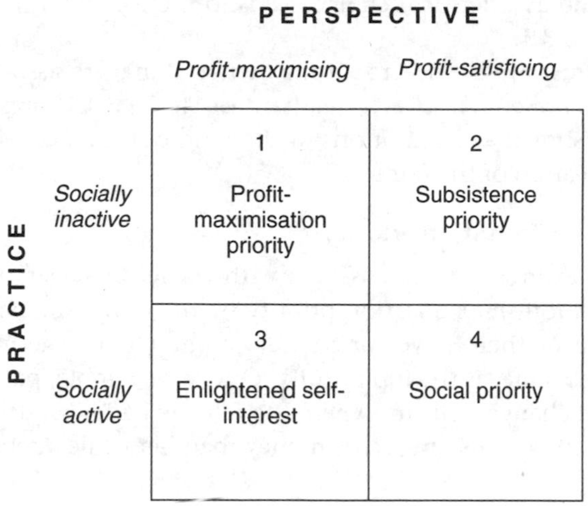

PRACTICE / PERSPECTIVE	*Profit-maximising*	*Profit-satisficing*
Socially inactive	1 Profit-maximisation priority	2 Subsistence priority
Socially active	3 Enlightened self-interest	4 Social priority

Figure 3.1 Frames of owner-managers (profit vs social activity)

owner-managers recognised the need for profit in order for their business to survive for comfortable retirement, or for their business to be sold on. Of key importance here is the distinction between whether profit earned should be the *maximum* possible, or whether a self-determined 'reasonable' alternative was acceptable to the owner-manager, or indeed preferable to profit-maximisation. The distinction between the motive of profit-maximisation versus profit-satisficing is the division represented on the horizontal axis.

On the vertical axis, note was taken of how active the respondents were in what might be termed issues which are not *directly* related to the commercial success of the business. These activities have been called non-commercial, or social activities. They include things like giving time or money from the business to charity, involvement with local schools or community groups, offering work experience opportunities, or contributing to caring for the environment. Each of these things has positive, non-pecuniary effects beyond the boundaries of the commercial operation of the business (some but not all may also be tax deductible). A distinction made was to what extent these social activities are seen as having positive effects on the financial side of the business – by fostering goodwill that will be cultivated into business opportunities at a future date, for example. The dominance of this enlightened self-interest approach to social activities compared to being socially active for its

own sake and as a personal choice, leads to the division on the vertical axis in Figure 3.1.

Below, illustrative evidence from owner-managers associated with the frame represented in each quadrant of Figure 3.1 is presented. The quotations shown are indications of the kind of evidence which led to the identification of the frames.

1. Profit-maximisation priority

One frame expressed in discussions with owner-managers is what we termed the profit-maximisation priority frame. Owner-managers sometimes spoke of their drive for money, as much of it as possible, as quickly as possible, as the top priority. One, for example, put this in the context of a change of heart, where she felt she had been driven to this because others were making more money than her while offering a lower-quality service:

> My aim at the moment is to make lots of money. It has changed. But the reasons it has changed is that I have seen so many people out there doing all sorts of crap and making money out there, so I think: 'Oh sod this'. It is a real change in emphasis though. It is a more aggressive stance. My stance is more aggressive now than it was. (BE2S, Management Consultancy, 4 employees)

Another, while describing the actions of a neighbouring firm, stressed that money, at the end of the day, was the key motivating factor. Whilst he relayed a story of his money-motivated neighbouring firm negatively, he then added that his organisation, too, would pursue profit over other motives:

> Money is money isn't it at the end of the day and everyone needs to earn a living for whatever. And if he can pick up extra work he will [*pointing to neighbouring firm*], and we would, unfortunately. (BE10S, Computer and Telecommunications Services, 8 employees)

The respondent suggests that money will always overcome other social motivations, for the neighbouring firm and for himself, although interestingly he comments that this is unfortunate. In this frame of small business life, however, the inevitability of taking financial opportunities that can be gained in the short term outweighs other factors.

The short-term perspective in this frame may not be motivated by avarice, but may be related to other pecuniary reasons, such as in the case below where the respondent is motivated by debt repayment to maximise profit:

> My personal motivation at the moment is to try and clear my debts that I have incurred over the years trying to run a business when people owe me a lot of money and have gone out of business and it has cost me a lot of money in refinancing and everything else... That's the motivation at the moment. (BE6M, Mechanical engineers, 6 employees)

Another owner-manager spoke of the drive to earn money in the short term as a forerunner for longer-term plans for retirement and in order to pay short-term costs associated with keeping children at university.

> *Interviewer*: What is keeping you in it?
> *Respondent*: At the moment, to retire.
> *Interviewer*: It is just financial?
> *Respondent*: Yes. We have two children who are still in university. (BE12S, Translators, 0 employees)

Two manufacturers spoke directly about the profit orientation of the company:

> I would like to see a more profit based company. I would like to see it moving on now... I would like to put more emphasis on the cash side of it. (BE14M, Manufacturer of moulds, 13 employees)
>
> We set out to be profitable and we are profitable and everything we have we own. (BE15M, Tape manufacturers, 11 employees)

Where the experience of running a small business is described in the financially orientated way, social issues tend not to be prioritised in the business life. This is not necessarily to suggest dishonesty in business transactions, or low-quality work. Small firm owner-managers, whose dialogue suggests an orientation to business is located in the first quadrant of Figure 3.1, may disregard social costs as having an inverse relationship with financial gain. Thus, these businesses conceptualise the profit motive and social objectives as being opposed. The reality of this perspective is a longstanding and unresolved point of debate in business ethics (Lynn, 1999).

2. Subsistence priority

Owner-managers sometimes framed their perspective on business as being based upon the establishment of long-term survival. They were primarily motivated by ensuring the survival of their firm and security of their livelihood. This 'frame' we have termed the subsistence priority.

One owner-manager, for example, stated that maintenance of a certain standard of living was the motive for doing business, not seeking high profits, which he considered would result in too high a personal cost:

> I am not driven by making more profits. You see those sorts of people who are driven by nothing but profit and give themselves ulcers and all sorts of things and there is no point, so I am driven by wanting to keep the house and home together, wanting a reasonable living but money in the bank isn't that important... Plain profit isn't the day-to-day motive although my standard of living is what I am doing it for, why I am working. If I could have the same standard of living by not working then that is what I would do. (BE19M, Rubber parts manufacturer, 12 employees)

The respondent, hence, made it clear that short-term financial gain was not an absolute priority. What prevailed was longer-term survival in order to ensure the standard of living.

Another respondent stated his interest in the long-term financial security for the company:

> Money is important, yes, and we are making a lot of money now, and the fact that we choose to reinvest in property and equipment is our choice, but if we weren't doing that we would be extremely wealthy, but we have chosen to buy into the long-term investment company approach. (BE7S, Marketing, 7 employees)

Those who consistently spoke in terms that represent a choice not to maximise profits but to focus on maintaining a longer-term perspective of ensuring the firm as a source of subsistence living, fitted into quadrant two of Figure 3.1. Survival in the long term is a key priority. Social concerns are not as important as simple survival. It is these firms that may be destined to grow in size, or more likely, simply 'bubble along' (BE14M, manufacturer of moulds, 13 employees), as one respondent put it. Ethics may be expressed in terms of ensuring long-term employment for employees and service for customers but is unlikely to go beyond that.

3. Enlightened self-interest

Respondents sometimes framed their motivations and actions in terms of being active in social issues, with the conscious positive influence that they perceive this will have on their profit and business in the long term. We have called this the enlightened self-interest frame.

The following respondent lucidly described his motivation of good business ethics, then qualifies his position by acknowledging that these things are good financially for business too. It should be noted that this is the same respondent that was cited above as showing evidence of the 'subsistence' frame. His comments here are not inconsistent, they simply demonstrate the differing views that can co-exist within respondents' descriptions of the priorities for their firms.

> I am motivated by good business ethics – trustworthy, honest, that sort of thing – and that's me personally but the partners certainly have the same beliefs. It is all about quality, doing it well as a company and everything above board and that goes too, [even though] you moan and groan, when you make a profit and you have to pay your percentage of taxes. Our belief was doing it by the book, proper paperwork and everything else. We formed a limited company status at the beginning. We weren't, obviously, aware of how far it was going to go but it put us in good stead, and also it is the fact that if you mislead or whatever, you have always got to be watching your back then. It is hard enough running a business and worrying about day-to-day stuff and keeping one eye over your shoulder, that sort of thing. (BE7S, Marketing, 7 employees)

The benefit of being trustworthy in the eyes of your customers, and the positive effect this can have on business from a financial perspective, were also illustrated thus. The respondents were asked 'Is it difficult to get new customers?'

> Most of them are quite fussy who they go to. You can't afford to upset them. They go to people they can trust because they haven't got time to be leaning over your shoulder all the time . . . I think that to survive and grow you have to have a good reputation. (BE11S, Architects, 5 employees)

> You can often pick up business by being honest with people, sometimes people come back to me. (BE4S, Fluid Power services, 1 employee)

Another respondent said:

> I think that if you want to build up business you have to do your best to be fair. People have to think you are fair or they are not going to come back to you. (BE8S, Antiques retailer, 0 employees)

Where the enlightened self-interest frame is adopted we meet the ethical debate of consequences versus motives. Owner-managers who take this perspective are not necessarily motivated by goodwill, but see good ethics as good public relations and a form of marketing. This is a perspective which we are more familiar with from large firms (Wyburd, 1998, pp. 140–2) but there was also some evidence of ethics as enlightened self-interest in the small firms in this sample.

4. Social priority

The final frame in the fourth quadrant of Figure 3.1 describes an experience of work as being more about a long-term choice of lifestyle than a profit and wealth maximising mechanism. As a result, social values and actions were integrated into the business life and took priority over maximising profit. One respondent, who has also been quoted in the profit-maximisation priority section, explains her perspective on this as follows:

> I do a lot of work and I spend a lot of my time doing voluntary work – I am a Registrar for my church and I have just been invited to be a Governor at a school. I am a director of another company and I give them an amount of free time in the year to do any consultancy help and support, so I will do a lot of things, what I call 'voluntary work', and I do it with just as much eagerness and effort and so on. It is important for me to have that balance, and one of the rules of working here is that one day a year, it is not a lot, but one day a year everybody has got to do something else for charity. I don't care what it is as long as it is something they choose they want to do . . . Use the resources, use the facilities and so on but it is important that I and they give something back.
>
> *Interviewer*: Why?
>
> Perhaps it is because I believe in God, or perhaps I realise . . . if it wasn't for my belief, my spiritual belief and that the fact that you don't get where you are without climbing up on someone's shoulder, so you can't not give something back because if you don't give what

> is there to grow for someone else? To me it is just a natural law of life – you take and you give and it is just terribly important. (BE2S, Management Consultancy, 4 employees)

The respondent thus puts her beliefs and actions in the context of religious beliefs and a spiritual perspective. A second respondent drew on his religious faith in business life as a motivating factor:

> From my point of view, although I am not perfect I have got a quite strong Christian faith that helps me a lot in business and I guess is a big priority in work when push comes to shove. (BE7S, Marketing, 7 employees)

Others also suggested that they had a wider view of life and that money was far from key in their objectives, such as in the following example:

> What I care about is whether I feel that I have done what is right for me, and that's what it is about. I can't tell you what guides those things. It could be parents, it could be schools, it could be religious teachings when you were a lot, lot younger, who knows, but that's what it is. I know for one thing I don't want to get to the top by treading on people on the way and I know by that I am never going to be a multi-multi millionaire. (BE9S, Computer Supply and Training, 38 employees)

The following respondent referred particularly to his employees when talking about the firm:

> They are my friends. I don't socialise with them outside work but I consider them to be my friends . . . In the remote circumstances that I win the Lottery on Saturday, not very likely, I couldn't just stop and go away, they are people. (BE19M, Rubber parts manufacturer, 12 employees)

Small firm owner-managers who understand their work to be a choice of lifestyle where social aspects are more important than high financial rewards fit into the fourth quadrant. Here, we might expect to find ethical and socially concerned and active business people. They appear to have control over their own lives and business. This is in stark contrast to employees or even directors of larger firms.

Discussion

Four frames for understanding the small business owner-manager's experience have been presented: profit-maximisation orientation, subsistence orientation, enlightened self-interest and social orientation. It should be stressed again that it would be difficult to assign each of the owner-managers to one of these framed positions alone. Interviewees often presented more than one frame when discussing the issues presented to them.

As some of the owner-managers voiced more than one perspective in the course of the interview it may be that their dominant frame of running a small business shifts over time, or according to the issue or circumstances under discussion. Some may prefer to adopt the social priority frame, but find that due to recession periods they are forced to take a more purely financial perspective. Others may strive for financial reward at the beginning of their small business career, and then decide that financial success does not bring the fulfilment expected. One, for example, said this:

> To be fair, money used to be a key thing – I wanted to be millionaire by the age of thirty until my brother got leukaemia and then things slightly changed. There is more to life than money. (BE9S, Computer Supply and Training, 38 employees)

This statement may show him moving from a finance priority frame to a social priority frame. Frame analysis should be seen as a dynamic representation of ways of understanding a particular experience, not a static tool.

Furthermore, owner-managers may simultaneously represent their firm's priorities through a number of different frames. Citations from the same respondent, such as the owner-manager of the Management Consultancy (BE2S), appear above. Frame analysis helps demonstrate the possible perspectives that an owner-manager may possess, not just the categorisation of owner-managers in a fixed typology. This contrasts with work by commentators such as Goss (1991). Goss suggested that management control in small firms might be categorised as Fraternalism, Paternalism, Benevolent Autocracy or Sweating (Goss, 1991, p. 73) and linked these to market conditions prevailing in different firms. Whilst this analysis complements such perspectives, unitary categorisations such as Goss's are exposed as inadequate by frame analysis which allows for the potential of multiple frames being evident in a single firm owner-manager's understanding of the experience of owner–managing a firm.

There has been an ongoing debate in small business research about the existence or otherwise of 'industrial harmony' in the small firm (Ram, 1999). The debate has ranged from the seminal Bolton Committee report (Bolton, 1971) which implied that the owner-manager was typically a benefactor and an active civic contributor, to later research which criticised these assumptions (Curran, 1991). More recent ethnographic-based studies such as those by Ram (1994) and Holliday (1995) have helped to contextualise the owner-managed firm further.

This research, however, focuses on what the owner-manager understands to be going on in his or her business; how they experience and explain, if only to themselves, what they are doing in relation to the world around them. It demonstrates the range of ethical positions that can be collected empirically from owner-managers' responses. It is not easy to associate different frames with different market conditions nor sectoral niches. The scope of voluntary human agency in framing one's ethical stance may be wider than is often assumed. 

The findings also resonate with the results of much small business research. Previous studies have made the distinction between various categories of firms, such as between the high-growth, profit-maximising firms, and the firms regarded as 'trundlers', 'lifestyle' or 'non-growth' businesses (Stanworth and Curran, 1986; Storey, 1994). It is this latter group of firms that are most numerous and are likely to be dominated by the subsistence priority frame when rationalising their business objectives. There is also an assumption behind the entrepreneurship and business development literature that businesses are likely to want to grow and expand and ultimately to maximise profit. Apart from the possible role of risk aversion in these decisions there is a likely relationship with ethical orientation. Those involved in policy and support for these businesses need to take these issues into account.

The notion that businesses take into account other objectives beside profit-maximisation will come as no surprise to many economists, though this is often dealt with in a similarly rationalistic manner (Holton, 1992, ch 2.). An alternative model of explaining the complexity of 'economic' behaviour and its social context comes from the sub-discipline of economic sociology. One concern of economic sociology and anthropology is the relationship between the social and the economic and the interplay between markets and morality (Holton, 1992; Dilley, 1992). Indeed, it is the alternative and sometimes contradictory moral codes deployed in livelihood generation that are being displayed within the research reported here. When discussing the complex relationship between economic life, culture and society the determinants are often difficult to distinguish. It is commonly only economists who accept the notion of a profit-maximising, optimising and rational *homo economicus* as an axiom of human behaviour. In contrast, others assert:

> Culture plays many roles in economic life: constituting actors and economic institutions, defining the ends and means of action and regulation, the relationship between means and ends. The term 'culture' refers to many different constructs: for example, scripts, metaphor, routine, category schemes, norms, values, rituals, institutions, schemas and frames, and switching rules. There is no more reason to believe that all these are implicated in any particular causal, constitutive, or regulatory relationship, or that all pull in the same direction in any empirical instance, than there is to assume that every aspect of 'social structure' simultaneously accounts for every 'structural effect'. (DiMaggio, 1994, p. 47)

In contrast with what we might expect from assumptions of business studies and economics, the least commonly presented frames in the data were the profit-maximisation priority frame and the enlightened self-interest frame. The most commonly presented frames in the data were the subsistence priority and the social priority perspectives. There might be some role for sampling biases. It is conceivable that the act itself of allowing someone free access to your time to be interviewed is not consistent with having a purely profit-maximising motive. Hence it could be that those who refused interview (only about 20 per cent) would have commonly framed themselves in the profit-maximisation priority perspective. This is one of the difficulties of non-response bias.

The enlightened self-interest frame, as alluded to previously, is one that is consistent with large firm business ethics perspectives. Since small firms are unlikely to have individuals who are active in marketing and public relations (Stokes, Fitchew and Blackburn, 1997), it is unsurprising that the conscious pursuit of goodwill for future commercial exploitation is not prevalent. Interestingly, the one company in the sample that most clearly vocalised the enlightened self-interest perspective, was a marketing firm (BE7S).

The subsistence frame suggests that for those running a business it can be just as much a means to an end, providing a source of income, as it is for employees of other organisations. The intention is not to be entrepreneurial or exceptionally wealthy, but to keep oneself, and perhaps colleagues, in employment. This is not a very romantic view of the business owner, and may be disappointing to policy-makers looking to small firms as the dynamic, entrepreneurial engine of the economy, but does seem to be an enduring reality in the UK economy.

The social priority frame, putting social issues over financial reward, goes beyond the subsistence frame. Owner-managers who adopt this frame may be dynamic and driven in their business life, but not necessarily for financial reward. They use their role in society to support social and ethical choices, and as owner-managers have the power to do that. This finding is in keeping with the acknowledgement that achievement of independence is a key motivation for running one's own business (Goffee and Scase, 1995, pp. 3–5).

The extent to which business owner-managers have a choice over which frame they adopt, and live their business lives, is key in this analysis. It may be considered that small firm owner-managers are pawns in a game over which they have no real control. This research indicates that in fact there is some autonomy through which an owner-manager can influence his or her position and frame. As one respondent put it succinctly:

> At the end of the day everybody is trying to do the same thing. They are just doing it with a different approach. Every business is being run for profit. Who takes that profit decides on the way that the business is being run but at the end of the day we have all got the same problems, we have all got the same suppliers, we have all got the same customers or we have all got the opportunity for the same customers, we have all got the opportunity of the same distributors, we all have the opportunity of the same people to employ. It is how we go about bringing those ingredients together to make our business. That is the only difference and that is down to the personality of the person who is running the business or the personalities running the business, that is the key thing. That is what it is all about. (BE9S, Computer Supply and Training, 38 employees)

It may similarly be assumed that socially active responses are only likely in a non-competitive environment. The following respondent describes how he has had some very difficult times but one of the reasons for keeping the firm going was for the sake of his employees.

> I have always been in business and it would have been easy for me to shut the business down over the years when you get bad debts, but

> you sit there and you say... to yourself it is not only going to be your family that has been affected but you are going to affect ten other people's lives as well. So if there is a way forward then there is a way forward although a lot of people don't do that... Morally I have an obligation and I hope that the people who work for you appreciate what you are trying to do. (BE6M, Precision Engineers, 6 employees)

The context, it seems, is not the only determining factor. Whether small firms can be said to operate strategically is a debatable point (Hutchinson and Chaston, 1994), but they are not subject to a 'deterministic' strategy, maintaining instead some degree of voluntarism in their actions (for elucidation, see Genus, 1998, pp. 3–11).

The findings discussed above go some way to helping with the future of business ethics research. We must be clear about the nature of small firms and the way in which they run their businesses. This is important not only for scholarly advancement, but also for the management of small businesses. An appreciation of one's own motives, and an understanding of the potential trade-offs, complementarity or conflicts between motives and perspectives allows the owner-manager to plan his or her investments and management. It may even be that a particular ethical orientation could be acknowledged in the firm's marketing and used as a unique selling point. Furthermore, it would be no bad thing if all of us understood our own ethical perspective on the world, as small business owners or otherwise, and acted in accordance with these perspectives. It is only in our actions that we can contribute to a more ethical business and social environment.

Conclusion

The findings presented here offer a platform for further investigation. In particular, we might consider how policy-makers could influence and persuade those who adopt different frames in running their business to be ethically responsible. It may well be that those most motivated by the profit-maximisation priority frame, subsistence priority frame, enlightened self-interest frame or social priority frame, can be differently stimulated to respond to social and ethical issues.

Those who are motivated by financial gain and profit-maximising may be stimulated to be more ethical by either legislation against anti-social activities, or perhaps by encouraging recognition that ethical behaviour can be profitable, and shifting their frame to the third quadrant of enlightened self-interest. Those who are aware of the profit that can be made from good ethics may be encouraged by the stimulation of customer and investor action in buying from ethical companies. The promotion of ethical standards in supply chain relationships may also be effective.

As has been mentioned in the discussion, in fact most small firms are likely to be dominated by the subsistence or social priority frames. Those in the second quadrant (subsistence frame) would again be most influenced by legal requirements which force them to consider social issues. Those who are already pursuing a socially and ethically responsible business style might be further encouraged by reward for their choices and information about the socially aware activities others are involved in.

Policy-makers should consider carefully how they would like small business-owners to contribute to society. In areas such as the promotion of employment rights, environmental performance and equal opportunities practices, careful consideration of the communication of such ideals is needed. They should not be presented, or perceived, as burdens on small enterprises, but as a social duty and morally desirable.

The sector differences in this research are inconclusive. Examples of quotations that illustrated any one of the four frames were available from both manufacturing and service companies. In this study there was no indication that, for example, manufacturers were more or less likely to be associated with the profit-maximisation priority frame than were service firms. Further research is needed that focuses more carefully on business sectors and the impact this can have on owner-manager perspectives of the firm.

The complexity of identifying predominant frames for each business owner should not be underestimated. The most likely situation is that policy-makers should acknowledge that several approaches are necessary to persuade owner-managers to change the direction of their business priorities in line with social awareness. An overriding misconception that needs to be addressed, however, is that owner-managers are overwhelmingly pursuing profit-maximisation. The reasons for being in business and running a firm are far more complex, and socially motivated, than purely financial reasons. The boundary between the third sector of social enterprises, often defined by their adherence to social objectives as their overriding concern, and the private sector, which is often attributed the overriding objective of profit-maximisation, may be a blurred one. Of course businesses have to watch their 'bottom line', as indeed social enterprises must do, but other objectives may, quite legitimately, be pursued in parallel.

Some might argue that policy-makers have no role to play in ethics and we should allow such things to come from within the individual. We suggest that this is simply not enough if we want to ensure that the gaps left by our current socio-economic system are to be filled more effectively in the future. However, policy-makers and the wider community should take note from this research that small businesses may not be the cut-throat profit-maximisers that popular media images would have us believe. In some of the cases uncovered here, small firms – at least from the owner-managers' perspective – were actually offering excellent examples of integrity and responsibility in business practice.

From the point of view of the small business owner, this research can help demonstrate that it is not 'unbusiness-like' to acknowledge social issues, but in fact is quite a normal perspective for small firm owner-managers. Raising awareness of this point may help owner-managers to think constructively about their role in society as part of their business activities. This may have 'bottom-line' influences if small firms become 'enlightened' in their utilisation of their ethical perspective as a marketing tool. It could be argued, however, that a much more fundamental culture shift in business practice could be a consequence of wider acknowledgement of ethics as a legitimate business consideration – confirmation that ethically and socially aware behaviour is not only 'socially desirable' and sometimes commercially desirable, but also a normal and acceptable (even expected) element of business life.

This research has helped to open up some of the questions surrounding priorities in the small firm and demonstrated that they go beyond the normal 'business' motivations of being profit-driven. Further research is required in order to fully understand the ethical orientation of SME owners and the complex range of factors that influence such behaviour. This would be more fruitful than an over-reliance on an imported philosophy based upon the notion 'economic man' which is not supported empirically.

Note

1. Thanks are due to Kingston University and the Institute of Business Ethics for funding the research reported on in this chapter and other related work. The support and advice of the staff of the Small Business Research Centre, Kingston University, and the School of Business and Management, Brunel University, have been greatly appreciated. This chapter was first published as the following article and has been reprinted with the kind permission of Henry Stewart Publishing: L.J. Spence and R. Rutherfoord, 'Social Responsibility,

Profit-Maximisation and the Small Firm Owner-Manager', *Small Business and Enterprise Development*, Summer, 8(2), (2001) 126–39.

References

Bain, W., 'Advancements in Empirical Business Ethics Research Methodologies', *British Academy of Management*, Annual Conference, Sept. 22, Milton Keynes (1993).

Bolton, J., *Report of the Committee of Inquiry on Small Firms*, Cmnd. 4811 (London: HMSO, 1971).

Bryman, A. and R. Burgess (eds), *Analysing Qualitative Data* (London: Routledge, 1994).

Business Ethics Quarterly, 'Ruffin Series Review of Business Ethics', *Business Ethics Quarterly*, 10(1), (2000).

Curran, J., 'Employment and Employment Relations', in *Bolton 20 Years On: The Small Firm in the 1990s*, J. Stanworth and J. Curran (eds) (London: Paul Chapman, 1991).

Curran, J. and R. Blackburn, *Small Firms and Local Economic Networks: The Death of the Local Economy?* (London: Paul Chapman, 1994).

Department of Trade and Industry, *Small and Medium Enterprise (SME) Statistics for the UK, 1998* Statistical Press Release P/99/662, 5 August 1999 (1999).

Dilley, R. (ed.), *Contesting Markets* (Edinburgh: Edinburgh University Press, 1992).

DiMaggio, P., 'Culture and Economy', in N. Smelser and R. Swedberg (eds), *Handbook of Economic Sociology* (New York: Sage, 1994) pp. 27–57.

Enderle, G., 'Towards Business Ethics as an Academic Discipline', *Business Ethics Quarterly*, 6(1), (1996) 43–65.

Friedman, M., 'The social responsibility of business is to increase its profits', *The New York Times Magazine*, September (1970) 13, 32–3, 122–6.

Genus, A., *The Management of Change: Perspectives and Practice* (London: Thompson, 1998).

Goffee, R. and R. Scase, *Corporate Realities: The Dynamics of Large and Small Organizations* (London: International Thomson Business Press, 1995).

Goffman, E., *Frame Analysis: An Essay on the Organization of Experience* (Boston: Northeastern University Press, 1974, reprinted 1986).

Goffman, E., *Forms of Talk* (London: Blackwell, 1981).

Goss, D., *Small Business and Society* (London: Routledge, 1991).

Harvey, B., 'Why Doing Good is Good Business', *The Director*, September (1988) 131–2.

Holliday, R., *Investigating Small Firms: Nice Work?* (London: Routledge, 1995).

Holton, R., *Economy and Society* (London: Routledge, 1992).

Howorth, C. and N. Wilson, 'Late Payment and the Small Firm: An Examination of Case Studies', *Small Business and Enterprise Development*, 5(4), (1999) 297–305.

Hutchinson, A. and I. Chaston, 'Environmental Management in Devon and Cornwall's Small and Medium Sized Enterprise Sector', *Business Strategy and the Environment*, 3:1, (1994) 15–22.

Liedtka, J.M., 'Exploring Ethical Issues Using Personal Interviews', *Business Ethics Quarterly*, 2(2), (1992) 161–81.

Lynn, M., 'Can Nice Guys Finish First?', *Management Today*, February (1999) 48–52.

Quinn, J.J., 'Personal Ethics and Business Ethics: The Ethical Attitudes of Owner/Managers of Small Business', *Journal of Business Ethics*, 16(2), (1997) 119–27.

Ram, M., *Managing to Survive – Working Lives in Small Firms* (Oxford: Blackwell, 1994).

Ram, M., 'Managing Autonomy: Employment Relations in Small Professional Service Firms', *International Small Business Journal*, January–March (1999) 13–30.

Small Business Research Centre, *Dialogue with Business Owners; Bi-annual Research into Their Motivations, Experiences and Views*, Horwarth Clark Whitehill/Kingston University, London (1997).

Spence, L.J., 'Does Size Matter? The State of the Art in Small Business Ethics', *Business Ethics: A European Review*, 8(3), (1999) 163–74.

Stanworth, J. and J. Curran, 'Growth and the Small Firm', in J. Curran, J. Stanworth and D. Watkins (eds), *The Survival of the Small Firm, Vol. 2* (London: Gower, 1986).

Stokes, D., S. Fitchew and R. Blackburn, 'Marketing in Small Firms: Towards a Conceptual Understanding', *Small Business Research Centre Research Monograph*, Kingston Business School, July (1997).

Storey, D., *Understanding the Small Business Sector* (London: Routledge, 1994).

Vyakarnam, S., A. Bailey, A. Myers and D. Burnett, 'Towards an Understanding of Ethical Behaviour in Small Firms', *Journal of Business Ethics*, 16(15), (1997) 1625–36.

Webley, S., *Codes of Ethics and International Business* (London: Institute of Business Ethics, 1997).

Wyburd, G., *Competitive and Ethical? How Business Can Strike a Balance* (London: Kogan Page, 1998).

4
SMEs, Social Capital and Civic Engagement in Bavaria and West London

René Schmidpeter and Laura J. Spence

In this chapter we report on a study on understanding social capital from the point of view of owner-managers and managing directors of a small sample of SMEs in two regions. While this excludes social capital generated by employees, we chose the owner-manager as being a likely major source of social capital opportunities for the firm. As Burt (2000, p. 282) notes, 'The social capital of people aggregates into the social capital of organizations.'

Empirical research has been completed to help improve our understanding of social capital and small and medium sized enterprises with particular reference to civic engagement. The research was qualitative in nature and had a comparative element, drawing on research conducted in Bavaria (Munich) and England (West London). These two areas have similarities in that they are wealthy and economically stable regions of Europe, with well-established small and medium sized enterprise infrastructures, and occupy an important role in the economy (Lauder *et al.*, 1994). We gained access to 5 garages, 5 marketing service firms and 5 food processing or manufacturing firms in each country from the *Yellow Pages* (*Gelbe Seiten* in Germany). The three sectors were identified as examples present in each region of a business-to-business service, a business-to-customer service and a manufacturer. These choices were made with a view to opening up the debate on social capital and SMEs which we expect to have sector-specific characteristics. This is in keeping with previous SME research where sectors have been found to make a critical difference (Curran and Blackburn, 2001, pp. 16–19).

In designing our research tool we drew on the wide literature of social capital to identify three levels which we used as stimulus questions: institutional links (e.g. trade group membership), network links (e.g. informal or formal local business group), and mutual trust relationships (e.g. with competitors). The work of Elinor Ostrom was particularly useful in identifying these levels of analysis (Ostrom and Ahn, 2001). We asked the respondents to discuss their 'commercial' contacts and their personal ones, since social capital is by its nature in the grey area not belonging to the commercial sphere alone (Habisch, 1999). We were interested in the local contacts of the respondents and their contributions to the local environment. In the study we investigated how institutions influence SME investment in social capital and how institutional change can be influenced by civic engagement and networks.

The international comparative aspect of the research required careful design and translation of the interview schedule. The German and English research partners interviewed together for as many of the interviews as was possible within the constraints of the project. The definition of SME was drawn from the European Union, as one of applied relevance in both Germany and the UK, i.e. independent firms with up to 250 employees (see Appendix A). However, it is recognised that sectoral differences were relevant in this. For example, the food manufacturing and processing companies tended not to be micro firms (fewer than 10 employees), whereas the marketing firms often operated with one or two people. In future research these differences should be acknowledged more closely.

Individual cases are referred to by their codes of SC (social capital project), UK or D (UK or Germany), 1, 2, 3, 4 or 5 (specific interview in series), F, G or M (Food manufacturing or processing, Garage, Marketing services). The line number of the original transcript is also referenced. The quotations from German respondents are translated into English in the text, with the original language shown in the endnotes. In accordance with research of this nature, the quotations are shown in their original raw state. The basic information relating to each company in the study is given in Table 4.1.

Analysis of the 30 transcripts resulted in the identification of themes relating to social capital for small and medium sized firms. Here we focus on those aspects of the data that help determine how social capital can be assessed with respect to SMEs. Relevant categories were found to be: formal engagement, networking within sectors, networking across sectors, volunteerism and giving to charity, and finally a focus on why people engage.

Table 4.1 Summary of participating firms

Code	*Year established*	*Number of employees*
SCD1M	1999	0
SCD2M	1998	1
SCD3M	1992	10
SCD4M	1994	10
SCD5M	1997	16
SCD1F	1985	30
SCD2F	1992	8
SCD3F	1902	65
SCD4F	1937	42
SCD5F	1881	16
SCD1G	1934	2
SCD2G	1986	4
SCD3G	1992	3
SCD4G	1990	4
SCD5G	1935	7
SCUK1M	1993	0
SCUK2M	1990	7
SCUK3M	1995	25
SCUK4M	1982	0
SCUK5M	1993	2
SCUK1F	1984	17
SCUK2F	1987	11
SCUK3F	1991	1
SCUK4F	1986	80
SCUK5F	1986	34
SCUK1G	1991	3
SCUK2G	1971	0
SCUK3G	1990	7
SCUK4G	1979	0
SCUK5G	1999	6

Formal engagement

None of the respondents in our research sample had roles in civic leadership, for example in local government, but a number were formally engaged with sector- or small firm-specific organisations. However, there are institutional differences between the two countries which influence associational membership. In the UK, for example, the owner-manager of SCUK4F, one of the larger food manufacture firms, had been a Director of the local Business Link. In Germany, the owner-manager of SCD3M had a role in the Chamber of Commerce. The Chambers system differs considerably between the two countries, with compulsory membership in

Germany (for a comparison of the UK and German Chambers systems, see Fallon and Brown, 1999). There is, however, still a role for voluntary engagement in both countries. In the case of the SCD3M owner-manager, this took the form of having a role in examining training programmes ((82) Prüfungsausschuss für Werbekaufleute). He is also responsible for one of the sub-groups, and is a member of the Board of the Chamber of Commerce.

Owner-manager of SCD5G served voluntarily on the Board of the Karosseriebauer-Innung (Body Work Association) for ten years (SCD5G, 65). This demonstrates a sector-specific example of formal engagement. When asked what the advantages of this were, he (SCD5G, 84) replies:

> In the first case, you are with these people, who you work together with, and you become friends, get known. It is, well, it is a kind of community.[1]

Some owner-managers interviewed did get involved, but in a more ad hoc manner. Garage owner-manager SCUK2G felt that he should speak up when there are issues he feels to be important. For example (SCUK2G, 162):

> I have been to council meetings and told them about developments that I don't consider right, I have been on the PTA around the school for about 10 or 12 years . . . (166) And so, I have always sort of taken pride in the community as it were.

In several cases, owner-managers stated an intention to become more involved in civic issues in the future (e.g. SCD1M, SCUK5F). This is of course difficult to evaluate, although it was often the case that they invoked the time needed to become established as a small firm as prohibitive to formal engagement outside of the firm. An example of this position was the owner-manager of a small marketing firm SCD1M:

> SCD1M (41) [I have not been involved] in voluntary institutions so far. The main reason is, there is no time for so-called secondary activities. This is also to do with the fact that all operative activities are still being carried out by myself or my brother, which is very time-consuming.[2]

If only examples of formal engagement were considered from our sample, a misleading impression of the extent of involvement in social issues of the SMEs concerned would be received. In fact, there were many varied cases of commitments of time and energy to civic and social issues, giving examples of social capital.

Networking within sectors

It has been found in previous research that SMEs often have ties with other firms, particularly other SMEs, in their sector (Spence *et al.*, 2001). Our study also reflects this finding, resulting in networks of firms in the same industry. Networks have been found by Burt to be an important source of social capital (2000, p. 282). This might be identified as bonding social capital. The form of these connections is wide-ranging, but included exchange of information, borrowing of equipment, recommendation and subcontracting. Previous work on garages has also found that they often have longstanding, cooperative informal links (Lloyd-Smith *et al.*, 1993, p. 125). The owner-manager of the food manufacturer SCD1F explains how these arrangements can come about:

> SCD1F (276–82) I've been collaborating for years with a couple of colleagues. But this came about because some of my employees dropped out or something like that. And then it went: 'You supply me with this . . . ' 'I supply you with that . . . ' Everybody saves himself something, those kinds of relationships do exist . . . but it is not collaboration on a bigger scale. It is just a sort of 'helping each other out', that everybody can take life a bit easier.[3]

One UK garage owner-manager told us how these relationships can result in concrete problem-solving assistance:

> SCUK2G (316) I was down getting an MOT down at [another local garage] yesterday and was discussing the job that I have had trouble with, with Bill and Ben and you sort of bounce off one another and they may have a suggestion that you haven't thought of, and you know, at the end of the day, I solved the problem that I have been batting [about] for about three weeks.

While we cannot claim that intra-sector collaboration is universal, all three of our sector samples included examples of within-sector collaboration in both the UK and Germany. On the whole we could say that this was most prevalent in garages and least in marketing firms. However, at least one example of no-contacts existed in the garages (SCUK1G) sample and one marketing firm had a wide network of marketing colleagues (SCD2M). In a literature review on networking produced for the Small Business Service, Blundel and Smith (2001, p. iii) also suggest that business networks have sector-specific characteristics.

Networking across sectors

Networking is not restricted to same-industry partners, of course. However, networking in cross-sectoral organisations was found to be less common in our sample. This might be identified as bridging social capital. Nevertheless, one of the examples given by owner-manager SCUK5F demonstrated how some problems and issues are non-sector specific and can produce useful rewards:

> SCUK5F (68) Yes, yes, sometimes it's always useful to network otherwise you think you are the only one with the problems and everyone else is fine, but it's only when you discuss that you find that yes, other people have similar problems and how they overcome them and sometimes you come up with the bright ideas because we all want to advertise for jobs or whatever but sometimes you always choose the wrong newspaper or the wrong media altogether, whereas by talking to people they would probably come up with some ideas. I mean recently I did that, they came up with a web idea which I'd never thought of because I thought I'm so regional that if I put on the web, then I'll probably get enquiries from Scotland [*laughs*] but it actually worked.

Networking with organisations from other sectors was most commonly found in our sample in cases of geographical proximity. Links were formed with neighbouring firms, often on the same industrial estate or street, rather than the broader local business community. For example, SCUK3G, a garage located in the high street of a very small town, organises a Christmas barbeque for neighbouring businesses, residents and customers:

> SCUK3G (156) All customers, anyone from off the street can come in and have a drink and eat or whatever, it's open to anyone really... (158). It's just for Christmas time when we all get together and have a few drinks and a bite to eat.

This apparently idyllic picture of village life is more interesting still when it is considered that the garage owner and his family did not live in the area but 20 minutes drive away. Furthermore, they are British Asians in the overwhelmingly white, Christian area where the business is located. This points to bridging social capital which reaches across community groups to arrive at new parameters of 'community'.

The owner-manager of the marketing firm SCD1M describes how he became friendly with the other people in the block in which the office is located. He says:

> SCD1M (266–8) You meet each other in the hallway. Or, if there is something concrete, someone comes, or you drop by. (292–4) I got a desk from the Casting Agent, they put it in for me. And then I offered it to the people from the Promotions Agency, because the colour didn't match after all, so they took it. Well, that is, that is basic neighbourliness.[4]

Garages often experienced parking problems for the vehicles they were working on, or found themselves in increasingly residential areas where conflicts have to be negotiated:

> SCD5G (139–41) The house over there was sold. Then it was renovated and decorated and sold as flats. And they showed the flats on Saturdays and Sundays, when there naturally wasn't any business going on. And then they moved in and on Monday suddenly a garage was there at work... And they were of course straight on the telephone, furious, and since then that is, I have indeed experienced a lot of anger.[5]

One of the most active examples of neighbourhood networking was given by the owner-manager of SCD3M. In this developing industrial estate, a group had been formed to deal with common local issues:

> SCD3M (236)... twice a year, that all owner-managers meet and have loose contact, a kind of platform... (256) One current issue: a kindergarten is going to start here on the property, over there. It will be a sort of nursery, so that it'll be easier for mothers to bring the kids with them, to leave them there and still be not far away from them.[6]

Interestingly, however, the group had been temporarily disbanded because one participant had hijacked it to forward his own agenda of complaints against the leaseholder. Management of such networks could be an issue for further research.

Volunteerism and giving to charity

Some of the owner-managers in our research were involved in voluntary work and gave their time and resources in areas other than traditional, formal 'civic' positions. In some instances, such as the owner-manager of SCUK5F, this was clearly directed and focused and drew on all the individual's networks and friends. He is a British Asian working in the food-manufacturing sector:

> SCUK5F (150) We actually formed a charity which was friends, groups of friends, we basically formed a charity group and this was in our youth, when we had a lot of time. Yes, we did a lot of charity work. Lately it's very much helping or supporting charities. We don't have any specific one but in the background there are plans, mainly to do.... because within the ethnic community there is a lot of issues with kidneys and it's one of the research guys based at the Hospital here whom I just met and got on with quite well. So that's the ambition, to basically do something specifically for kidney patients because there are a lot of people struggling for dialysis machines and they don't have enough room for that, so that's the only thing. (152) Basically among my friends we have quite a few and these are friends for eighteen, twenty years. We have got a very good network, we meet, everybody meets and whatever, so if someone initiates then we get this support, instantaneous support.

Others use their skills directly for good causes. Owner-manager SCDIM had the idea of setting up a donations portal, using his know-how and business skills directly:

> SCD1M (177–9) There is a social institution I'm planning to get involved in. It is not an association, it is a sort of institution that can be termed a donation portal (on the internet). It is a portal, where several charities are presented. And I'd like to get directly involved in there. It's not that I have taken concrete steps, yet, but I want to become active soon.[7]

Owner-manager SCUK3G clearly made the link between donating time and money to the local community and the possible financial rewards to the business. Amongst other things he was heavily involved with the local football club. Here, we can assume that the local customer base has an influence:

> SCUK3G (123) When you're involved in a small, local community, I would think I must pick up 35–40 per cent business through that contact, probably more, but then again I've missed spending a lot of time with it, so it more or less pays for it that way. Bringing, involving local community, if any local sponsors like the school needs money, I will help them for whatever they're doing. There's a little bowling alley round the back here in [*place name*], so I do a little bit of sponsorship for them. I've done a big sponsorship for a guy, a one-man band, one of my customers, £1,000 sponsorship for his car, he's in the racing which comes on telly. We don't advertise in the paper for work, we spend our money, our marketing side through sponsorship. That's the only bit of . . . advertising we do. So that's how we get the business.

Voluntary work and giving were sometimes carried out by the partners of the owner-manager, usually the wife, whose time is available as a result of the owner-manager being the main breadwinner. This involvement could also bring business benefits on occasion. Examples of this are given below:

> SCUK2G (342) My wife runs the local cancer support drop-in centre . . . she knows a lot of people, I know a lot of people through her. (362) She is fully into the local community, completely really because she is meeting people all the time not only for professional reasons but also to support families.

> SCUK5F (142) I haven't managed to have much time but my wife is fairly active [in the local community] so yes I just follow her.

The importance of looking at the whole family unit when considering the social capital of the owner-manager is one to keep in mind for future research.

Why do people get engaged?

In order to consider how to encourage civic engagement, it is necessary to know why it is that people contribute – what motivates them to be a member, build links, volunteer and develop mutual trust relationships. In short, why do people engage?

Some invoked notions of community and a feeling of wanting to 'give something back':

> SCD2M (284) Why do I do it? Because I think everybody needs to have at least one social project.[8]

> SCUK4F (241) I think you do use the local community, you have got to give something back if you can if you like, perhaps that sounds a little bit arrogant I don't know but it is the way it is, I just felt that it was a good idea to put something back into the local community.

Others considered that their personality type determined it. For example, when asked why they get involved and are engaged in activities outside the firm, some respondents answered as follows:

> SCUK5F (156) I as a person, I just set goals in life and whilst you are young there is only so much you can do and I've got this business growth which I want to be something and then I want to do something for the community and I think it's very much a personal thing. Some people are quite happy, they couldn't be bothered, whereas I like challenges and that's what I am doing.

> SCUK2G (316) Of course, I mean, you don't go through life without meeting people do you? Making friends. I think I am a fairly amicable sort of person and if I think a person, not that I use people, but if I think something is interesting or you know that people have got something that I haven't then I will go and speak to them and learn from them, you know

Indeed personality type was invoked as a reason why not to be involved:

> SCD1M (175) [I am] Not a member of an association, I'm basically not the type of person that is interested in associational activities or membership. It's more of an individualism.[9]

However, we must be careful in the conclusions we draw on the basis of personality type and avoid making unsubstantiated causal links. Lloyd-Smith *et al*. (1993, p. 130) have suggested that a plausible case can be made for garage owners being predominantly 'genial, trusting and outward-looking', which concurs with our findings. However, in their research they find that rather than particular personality types choosing appropriate sectors to work in, sectors tend to determine behaviour.

Some owner-managers identified the benefits that came from engagement, which emerge over the long term:

> SCD3M (138) Well, I've been wondering about it as well, what the benefits are. Links, perhaps. I see it more in the long-run, say, you generate through the work you're doing there contacts and create a network, and all that on a reputable level, which is not necessarily linked to the actual business. Especially with the [particular] Association, it was a sort of development that started when I was a student. They just approached me and asked whether I'd like to get involved in the Munich regional club.[10]

The owner-manager of the largest firm in our sample, SCUK4F, suggested that he sought camaraderie from his involvement in outside groups and networks. His observation may well be related to the fact that with a medium sized firm it is difficult to be 'one of the team' in the same way that may be possible with a small firm.

> SCUK4F (241) I think really, what probably drives it all is the thought that if you are the Manager it is a lonely place. I mean, it is a very isolated place to be. It comes from your background whatever it may be.

The empirical evidence presented above confirms that social capital can be identified in the activities of SMEs. In the following section we draw on some of the theoretical aspects of social capital introduced in Chapters 1 and 2 in relation to our empirical findings for small and medium sized enterprises in Germany and the UK.

Discussion

The interactions of German and British businesses with their environment vary according to differences in the formal institutions and legal system in both countries (Habisch and Schmidpeter, 2001). Kitching and Blackburn (1999, p. 629) have argued that 'the British industrial order is characterised by the social isolation of firms: businesses have to rely on their own individual resources to achieve their objectives'. In

Germany, some relationships are more institutionalised, such as that between business and the education system called the 'Duale Ausbildungssystem' (vocational education system). Apprentices thus receive on-the-job training alongside a college education and resulting qualification. As a result of this system the structural opportunity for German managers to train young people and interact with educational institutions arises. Results are not conclusive, however – not all our German respondents offered apprenticeships, citing the cost of paying for someone who is studying part of the time as one of the reasons. A few of our UK respondents offered training and apprenticeship voluntarily, too, and had contact with education institutes.

The lower number of SMEs in Germany may be linked to the fact that the legal preconditions for starting a business are higher than in the UK. This, and the obligatory membership of the Chamber of Commerce, leads to a base line of more formalised relationship between SMEs and business associations in Germany compared with the UK. This greater tendency for German SMEs to be members of associations (*Verbandswesen*) has also been found in other studies (Kitching and Blackburn, 1999, p. 625). Considering the Chamber of Commerce perspective particularly, the German system potentially enables advantages such as 'comprehensive local business membership, balanced representation of local economic interests, legitimacy as the voice of local business' (Fallon and Brown, 1999, p. 292). This credibility is not a panacea for SMEs – there are also complaints of overly bureaucratic processes and lack of awareness of services available – but there remains an institutional framework for representing all SMEs at a local and national level, which has the potential at least for furthering SME needs in Germany. Only a couple of the UK sample were Chamber of Commerce members, the others not seeing membership as relevant or valuable to their business. Chambers of Commerce do not have a full legitimate mandate to speak on behalf of small and medium sized enterprises in the UK. The Federation of Small Businesses is an alternative association, but none of the SMEs in our sample were members. Business Links also purport to represent SMEs, but again only a couple of our SMEs had been involved with Business Links. This lack of representation of SMEs is a barrier to the institutional support of them in the UK. There is no single organisation that can credibly deliver policy messages to SMEs. Imperfect though the Chamber of Commerce system in Germany might be, there is at least potential for wide cross-sectoral SME communication.

In addition to the differences in the structural systems of both countries, the distinctions between the sectors is also significant. Rather than cross-sectoral groups, SMEs in both Germany and the UK are likely voluntarily to join sector-based groups. These took the form of trade associations, supplier networks and informal contacts. These sector groupings are appropriate for joint problem-solving and representation since organisations in the same sector experience similar business issues and challenges.

We find that marketing firms tend to have relatively little engagement with the local community, making use of new technologies such as the Internet and email to integrate in different ways and to operate remotely (e.g. SCD1M and SCUK1M). Garages tend to draw their customer base from neighbours and build up a local network, hence it is relatively natural that they come into contact with local issues. All the garages we spoke to, for example, had to deal with issues of parked cars and at some stage had needed to negotiate with residential and business neighbours about this. Food manufacturers and processors tended to be the larger firms in the sample, and perhaps naturally issues around employees came to the fore. Employees tend to come from the neighbouring area, and, through them, employers become engaged in the local community; as SCUK4F noted, supporting the local community benefits the business in the long run because of reputational factors making it 'easier to get people to employ' (442). It looks likely that similarities within sectors is at least as strong a tendency as national characteristics in our sample.

Considering the structure of political organisation and location it is also interesting to note the influence that the right to vote on a local level can have on the engagement of business people. In Germany and the UK a person is only allowed to vote on the local level in the area where he/she lives. If the business is not in the living area, engagement need not be due to a lack of personal awareness of the problems, but also due to the limited opportunities to participate in the local political system (see SCD2M). However, where local employment is important, association with the business location and concern for the local community can come to the fore, as in the case of SCUK3G. Putnam (2000, p. 85) has noted the shift from local (residential) communities to vocational communities, but it seems that there may be a limit to this for some SME owner-managers not living where they work.

In terms of networks, relationships to other SMEs are important in combating competitive pressure. This finding correlates with earlier work on SMEs and competitor relations (Spence *et al.*, 2001). These relationships have the potential for compensating for the lack of size and associated loss of economy of scale and security which is often a characteristic of SMEs. The mutually beneficial support and benefits may take the form of a broader range of products and services to customers, faster and more flexible response times and the purchase of materials and services in an informal, ad hoc way without undue bureaucratic constraints (Goffee and Scase, 1995, p. 18).

Civic engagement of owner-managers is not always business-orientated. Often local involvement offers a pleasant change of focus and a different challenge. A particularly clear case of this was the owner-manager SCUK3G, who is heavily involved in a local football club as Chairman. He goes as far as to imply that he could not be successful in his business if he did not have this other engagement, although of course it also takes up his time and energy. Nevertheless business resources (computer, organisational know-how, etc.) are used and new business contacts can build up indirectly through these civic activities. The networks thus seem to be multifaceted, which contributes to different goals and sometimes leads to unintended results that contribute to business and society. However, we must be careful here. SME owner-managers are already busy people. Time spent away from the business may have positive business results but may also have negative impacts on the firm if only in terms of time not invested therein.

The question of intention is an important one. Only one or two of the cases which we studied were orientated towards networking purely for the purpose of building the business (e.g. SCUK5M). Many of the examples of civic engagement had no impact whatsoever on the business except for time and energy lost to it. Since it has been found elsewhere that profit-maximisation (Goffee and Scase, 1995, pp. 3–5; Chapter 3, this volume) is not the key motivator of small firm owner-managers, we should not be surprised by this. Owner-manager SCUK1M, for example, feels quite firmly that friends and business should not be mixed. On the other hand, it often happened that business contacts came anyway, even when that was not the motivation – for example, SCD3F met his sales manager at the golf course. Many of the owner-managers acknowledged that their engagement, although not motivated by business reasons, often resulted in positive business outcomes. There is a deeper issue here about the lack of 'home/work' distinction for the SME owner-manager. The owner-managers in our study found that they had a responsibility to employees and customers, even competitors, beyond 'business', i.e. a personal obligation and connection.

The major restriction to engagement is time and perceived opportunity for 'civic engagement'. SME owner-managers are extraordinarily busy people. When asked what they would need in order to be able to become more engaged they all answer 'more time'. However, this is perhaps a superficial perspective. Some of the respondents clearly had very active and committed working lives but still found time to be engaged in civic issues, while others did not. It is unclear what makes the difference in these situations. Several respondents talked about the 'type of person' they were as being prone to getting involved or alternatively preferring to sit on the sidelines. Those who were not engaged often said that they planned to become more so in the future, although it is impossible from our study to know whether this is wishful thinking or a serious intention, and subsequent action!

A related perspective here is the role that the marriage partner plays. Most of our respondents were men, and several of them talked about their wives as being the one who gets involved in civic issues. In this way it is as if the time spent by the husband on the business frees up the time the wife has to invest in social capital. This gendered perspective may change as traditional roles become less clearly defined. The work/leisure distinction is very porous for the SME owner-managers in this study.

Local and business related problems can sometimes be alleviated by SME engagement, but there are problems that are not likely to be in their scope. Few SMEs engage on an international or state level, where SMEs are very dependent on the decisions of politicians. Exceptions in our sample were the two largest food manufacturing SMEs, SCD3F and SCUK4F. The respective owner-managers had both spent years building up communications with national and international level politicians and partners. It is unclear how these social networks can be passed on with succession of the firm. The question of 'inheriting' social networks and continuing to reap repositories of social capital becomes complex, linking to the difficulty of smooth succession of small firms. (See Chapter 5 for further discussion on this.)

Informal networks were indeed found to be important for gaining access to necessary information to run a business. Sometimes these useful connections can subsidise formal information provision afforded to members of a business association. Informal work–friendship groups are also a source of reflection on how other business people do their work, insider information on the direction of business trends, and wider opinion. Thus it helps to gather and sort out information that affects or will affect the way business is done. Also it is an important mechanism for word-of-mouth marketing and thus informal sanctioning that helps to avoid bad practice through informal reputation management. All our SMEs gave word-of-mouth marketing as their main means for gaining new business.

It should be noted that we are not suggesting that association membership and networking is the way forward for all SMEs. However, we do feel that there are clear benefits from appropriation of goodwill from one type of engagement into other issues. Bennett (1999, p. 593) has argued that the 'role of associations in generating growth depends on their ability to improve the performance of individual firms through offering selective benefits (such as information and advice), through collective supports to their whole sector or members, and through actions on behalf of others (such as self-regulation)'. Here he assumes that SMEs want to grow, which is not always the case, and of course we cannot assume that all associations provide such an excellent service. The cost of membership was also a factor for our respondents (e.g. SCD2M); indeed, it has been found elsewhere that SMEs evaluate the costs and benefits of associational membership, and are carefully calculative (Bennett, 1999, p. 606). The voluntary versus compulsory tendency towards association membership in the UK compared with Germany is bound to have influence on trust levels and social commitment, and in turn social capital.

To conclude, we have found some fascinating indications of difference in social capital building by small firms[11]. The trajectories of difference are noticeable in German/UK comparisons but most significant between sectors. This has important implications for policy issues and future research opportunities, which are elaborated on in the concluding chapter of this book.

Notes

1. Original German: 'In erster Linie mal, du bist mit diesen Menschen, die wo du da zusammenarbeitest bist du befreundet, bekannt. Das ist, das ist halt irgendwie eine Gemeinschaft.'
2. Original German: 'In in freiwilligen, Institutionen bisher nicht. Der Grund ist vor allem, dass die Zeit derartige, ich nenn' es mal sekundäre Tätigkeiten nicht da ist. Das hat auch zu tun eben mit der Situation, das momentan noch alles, auch die operativen Sachen, von von mir oder meinem Bruder gemacht werden, was sehr zeitintensiv ist.'
3. Original German: 'Ich arbeite seit x Jahren mit ein paar Kollegen zusammen . . . Es ist aber mehr durch Problematik im Betrieb entstanden, wir mir die Leute ausgefallen sind und sonst irgendwas. Und da hat man gesagt 'Gut, du lieferst mir das' 'Ich liefer dir das' . . . Jeder spart sich irgendwo ein bisschen was, solche Verbindungen bestehen schon . . . Aber das artet nicht in große Aspekte aus. Das ist eigentlich nichts anderes als wie ein Unter-dem-Arm-greifen, dass der andere oder jeder ein bisschen, das Ganze ein bisschen leichter nehmen kann.'

4. Original German: 'Man trifft sich auf dem Gang . . . Oder, oder wenn man 'ne konkrete Sache hat, kommt man auch, geht man auch vorbei. (292–4) Ich hab Schreibtische von der von der Casting-Agentur bekommen, habe sie mir reingestellt. Dann haben sie mir nicht gefallen, weil die weil die dann doch farblich nicht gepasst haben. Dann hab ich sie denen von der von der Promotions-Agentur angeboten, dann haben die die genommen . . . Also das ist so, Basis Basisnachbarschaftshilfe.'
5. Original German: 'Sind da, gerade da drüben, das Haus, das ist verkauft worden. Dann wurde das ganze Haus renoviert und hergerichtet und lauter Eigentumswohnungen verkauft. Und die haben denen die Wohnungen am Samstag, Sonntag gezeigt, wo da natürlich kein Betrieb war. Und dann sind die eingezogen und am Montag ist da plötzlich eine Werkstatt, die gearbeitet hat . . . Und die haben natürlich dann gleich, waren am Telefon und Mordsärger und seitdem das da so ist, habe ich da schon einen Ärger hier drin.'
6. Original German: 'zweimal im Jahr, dass sich alle Geschäftsführer treffen und man so lose Kontakt hat, so als Plattform. (256) Was was jetzt diskutiert wird: wir kriegen 'nen Kindergarten hier auf's Gelände. Also so'n, hier ja, da drüben. Da kommt so 'ne Kinderkrippe 'rein, so dass also Mütter es einfach leichter haben, mal die Kinder mitzunehmen, hier abzugeben und man ist trotzdem nicht weit weg.'
7. Original German: 'Es gibt eine eine soziale Einrichtung, wo ich geplant habe, mich mehr zu betätigen. Das ist aber kein Verein, das ist eine Institution, die eine, man kann's am einfachsten beschreiben mit einem Spendenportal. Das ist eine eine ein Portal, wo Spendenangebote dargest präsentiert werden. Und . . . eben direkt dort tätig werden können. Und da, das ist jetzt noch nicht so, dass ich da etwas unternommen hätte, aber es ist 'ne, wär für mich das das nächste, was ich an an Tätigkeiten will.'
8. Original German: 'Warum ich das mache? Weil ich denke, dass jeder, ich sage, jeder braucht mindestens ein "social project"'
9. Original German: 'nicht nicht in einer Vereinigung, ich bin auch grundsätzlich vom Typ her nicht nicht sehr interessiert an Vereins Tätigkeiten oder Vereinmitgliedschaften. Ist mehr so'n Individualismus.'
10. Original German: 'Also, das habe ich mich auch schon paar Mal gefragt, was das wirklich bringt. Eventuell Kontakte. Ich sehe es eher langfristig, das man einfach sagt, man generiert über die Arbeit, die man da macht, einfach Kontakte und entwickelt ein Netzwerk und das Ganze auf 'ner seriösen Ebene, die jetzt nicht mit tatsächlichem Business zu tun hat. [Pause] Also das war, also speziell beim beim XXXsverband war es eben von meinem Studium her da bei der, bei der XX einfach so 'ne Entwicklung. Die hatten mich da mal angesprochen, ob ich da den Club München mitbetreuen würde.'
11. The results of this research project have been published elsewhere, including Spence and Schmidpeter (2003) and Spence *et al.* (2003)

References

Bennett, R., 'Business Associations: Their Potential Contribution to Government Policy and the Growth of Small and Medium-Sized Enterprises', *Environment and Planning C: Government and Policy*, 17(5), (1999) 593–608.

Blundel, R. and D. Smith, *Networking* (London: Small Business Service, 2001).

Burt, R., 'The Network Entrepreneur', in R. Swedberg (ed.), *Entrepreneurship: The Social Science View* (Oxford: Oxford University Press, 2000), pp. 281–307.

Curran, J. and R. Blackburn, *Researching the Small Enterprise* (London: Sage, 2001).

Fallon, G. and R. Brown, 'Public Law Status Chambers of Commerce: Does Britain Need Them?', *Small Business and Enterprise Development*, 6(3), (1999) 287–98.

Goffee, R. and R. Scase, *Corporate Realities: The Dynamics of Large and Small Organizations* (London: International Thomson Business Press, 1995).

Habisch, A., 'Sozialkapital', in W. Korff (ed.), *Handbuch der Wirtschaftsethik*, Band 4 (Gutersloh: Guterloher Verlaghaus, 1999), pp. 472–509.

Habisch, A. and R. Schmidpeter, 'Social Capital, Corporate Citizenship and Constitutional Dialogues – Theoretical Considerations for Organisational Strategy', in A. Habisch, H.P. Meister and R. Schmidpeter (eds), *Corporate Citizenship as Investing in Social Capital* (Berlin: Logos-Verlag, 2001), pp. 11–18.

Inkeles, A., 'Measuring Social Capital and its Consequences', *Policy Science*, 33, (2001) 245–68.

Kitching, J. and R. Blackburn, 'Management Training and Networking in Small and Medium Sized Enterprises in Three European Regions: Implications for Business Support', *Environment and Planning C: Government and Policy*, 17(5), (1999) 621–35.

Knack, S. and P. Keefer, 'Does Social Capital Have an Economic Payoff? A Cross-Country Investigation', *Quarterly Journal of Economics*, 112(4), (1997) 1251–88.

Lauder, D., G. Boocock and J. Presley, 'The System of Support for SMEs in the UK and Germany' *European Business Review*, 94(1), (1994) 9–16.

Lloyd-Smith, S., K. Dickson and A. Woods, 'The Industrial Divide in Services: Technological Innovation, Co-operation and Competition in Small Employment, Design, Plant Hire Firms and Garages', in F. Chittenden, M. Robertson and D. Watkins (eds), *Small Firms Recession and Recovery*, Institute for Small Business Affairs (London: Paul Chapman, 1993) pp. 113–37.

Onyx, J. and P. Bullen, 'Measuring Social Capital in Five Communities', *Journal of Applied Behavioural Science*, 36(1), (2000) 23–42.

Ostrom, E. and T. Ahn, 'A Social Capital Perspective on Social Capital: Social Capital and Collective Action', Gutachten für die Enquete-Kommission, '*Zukunft des Bürgerschaftlichen Engagements*', Kdrs. Nr. 14/107 (Berlin, 2001).

Paldam, M., 'Social Capital: Definition and Measurement', *Journal of Economic Surveys*, 14(5), (2000) 629–51.

Putnam, R., *Bowling Alone: The Collapse and Revival of American Community* (New York: Simon & Schuster, 2000).

Spence, L.J. and R. Schmidpeter, 'SMEs, Social Capital and the Common Good', *Journal of Business Ethics*, 45(1–2), (2003) 93–108.

Spence, L.J, R. Schmidpeter and A. Habisch, 'Assessing Social Capital: Small and Medium Sized Enterprises in Germany and the UK' *Journal of Business Ethics*, 47(1), (2003) 17–29.

Spence, L.J., A-M. Coles and L. Harris, 'The Forgotten Stakeholder? Ethics and Social Responsibility in Relation to Competitors', *Business and Society Review*, 106(4), (2001) 331–52.

5

Social Capital as a Long-Term Resource Among Ethnic Networks: The South Asian Business Community in Britain

Shaheena Janjuha-Jivraj

In this chapter,[1] research on social capital and embedded networks for first- and second-generation members of Asian small firms in Greater London is presented.

Resources such as financing, labour, information and other forms of support have often been cited as examples of social capital available to ethnic, and in particular Asian,[2] businesses. The support offered by the Asian community through extended family members and kinship ties has been highlighted as a means by which Asian businesses are able to negotiate significant competition in their markets. Business support within the Asian business community originated informally through the bonds of sub-groups. For many groups this was strengthened by migratory experiences from the Indian sub-continent to the United Kingdom (in some cases via East Africa). As members of the community settle and achieve varying degrees of integration with the mainstream population, it is expected that reliance on the voluntary ethnic community will diminish over time (Modood, 1992). This chapter considers the sustainability of voluntary networks within the British Asian business community by exploring the evolving notions of social capital amongst two generations actively involved in family businesses. In order to discuss the nature of social capital amongst progressive generations within this ethnic group the discussion in this chapter is based on Portes's (1998) critique of various sources of social capital. This is supported by a brief exploration of the recent work on embedded networks.

Social capital

Literature on ethnic entrepreneurship has acknowledged the considerable influence of informal support structures in providing various forms of support to businesses (Werbner, 1990; Ram, 1994a; Mattausch, 1998; Fadahunsi *et al.*, 2000). Business networks often develop around the entrepreneurs' personal networks, building on their social capital to generate mutually beneficial relationships satisfying a combination of business and social needs (Marger, 2001). Brehm and Rahn (1997) define social capital as 'the web of cooperative relationships between citizens that facilitates resolution of collective action problems' (p. 999). In the same paper the authors argue that different experiences nurture social capital within communities, including 'cultural patterns', reinforced by Adler and Kwon (2002) in their synthesis of approaches to this subject. Hite (2000) divides the notion of personal relationships into three distinct types based on varying degrees of emotional proximity and involvement with the network. Kloosterman *et al.* (1999) describe the combination of social and professional networks primarily for economic benefit as 'mixed embeddedness' and attribute this interaction predominantly to ethnic communities. They argue that embedded networks of individuals are not limited to one's ethnic group, but incorporate resources available through the wider community. Rather than arguing that ethnic-based resources have a limited lifespan dependent on the degree of integration achieved by members, this view combines the strengths derived from membership in the ethnic community with wider opportunities:

> we propose the use of a more comprehensive concept of mixed embeddedness that aims at incorporating both the co-ethnic social networks as well as the linkages (or lack of linkages) between migrant entrepreneurs and the economic and institutional context of the host society. (Kloosterman *et al.*, 1999, p. 252)

These experiences of group cohesion reinforce Bourdieu's (1985, cited in Portes, 1998) approach to social capital and in particular the benefits that accrue through cultural capital: ability to exploit resources through contacts with individuals or experts. When applied to the migrant Asian community, this approach has some validity; for many members, the access to cultural capital was limited to the parameters of the sub-group. For the first generation, access to resources beyond ethnic sub-groups was largely inhibited by the reticence of the migrant community to achieve further integration, predominantly as a response to the wider hostility of the indigenous population (Ram, 1994b). This inability to integrate with the wider community resulted in greater group cohesion. Portes (1998) developed this notion further. His critique of work by Marx encompassed the process of solidarity as '[an] emergent product of a common fate' (1998, p. 28). This portrayal of group cohesion is as applicable to ethnic migration as it is to class emergence amongst the industrial proletariat. Within the same context, Portes (1998) argues that the altruistic nature of donors is finite, bounded by the constraints of wider community resources. The large wave of economic migrants from the 1972 Ugandan expulsion entered Britain with limited financial capital. South Asian migrants from other areas hoped that Britain would fulfil their expectations, enabling them to return home a success. Overall, in terms of cultural capital, the strength of the Asian community lay in their entrepreneurial abilities, education and willingness to provide support in almost any form for their kinsmen. The strength of this support meant that amongst many groups longstanding divisions, based primarily on religion, were forsaken to achieve solidarity for survival:

> [migrants] have retained the unity given by their regional culture, language and kinship ties. Indian communities overseas are found organized to this day on this recognition of regional culture and language rather than an all India basis. (Desai, 1963, p.1)

The final aspect of social capital to be considered at this stage focuses on the obligation generated through such exchanges. Durkheim's (1984, cited in Portes, 1998) work on classical foundations of social integration emphasises the context of donors and recipients rather than direct reciprocity. This scenario applies particularly to the migrant Asian community. Various forms of exchange are offered without expecting direct repayment; instead, benefits may be accrued through indirect offerings, such as improved status amongst the collective. The pressure on members to behave in a socially responsible manner is highlighted by Portes (1998), who stresses the power of the community group on minimising deviant behaviour. The development of ethnic enclaves meant many migrants lived and worked within a close spatial network, leading to very close ties and strong forms of community control. The forms of support offered to community members ranged from temporary dwellings to short-term loans, from exchanging information on business ideas to acting as referees for bank loans. Accepting loans would lead to the most direct form of obligation of repaying the money either through a predetermined plan or informal agreement. The other examples stated above, however,

did not necessarily entail direct reciprocity. Instead, the offer to help was based on the assumption that the recipient would continue the chain of support by providing help to the next family/individual who arrived requiring assistance (Ballard and Hurst, 1994). This fulfils Portes's (1998) description of social integration:

> social capital is not contingent on direct knowledge of their benefactor, but on membership in the same group ... In other words trust exists in this situation precisely because obligations are enforceable, not through recourse to law or violence but through the power of the community. (1998, p. 28)

Asian entrepreneurship

The impact of donors being elevated to a higher status is particularly applicable within the Asian migrant group. Experiences of migration meant that many members found that the positions of status they had occupied in East Africa or India were denied to them in Britain by blocked employment opportunities (Lyon, 1971–3; Hiro, 1991). Entrepreneurship provided a means of negotiating these barriers, as described in Srinivasan's (1992) blocked upward-mobility thesis. Having achieved a position of relative stability, business families then offered support to other community members and through this helped other families to progress economically and socially. The emphasis on community status enabled Asian migrants to reclaim some of the importance they experienced prior to migration (Janjuha-Jivraj and Woods, 2002). The main components of embedded networks are: trust, personal relationships, dyadic interaction and social capital (Hite, 2000). These factors are all relevant to the various layers of relationships that develop within ethnic communities. The discussion in this chapter focuses in particular on the aspects of personal relationships and social capital of first-generation ethnic entrepreneurs and how these evolve with the settlement and development of the second generation. Most work on social or cultural capital emphasises the relationships between individuals and their immediate and extended network.

First-generation Asian migrants

Work cited in this discussion has emphasised the importance of group solidarity generated as a result of sharing common experiences. Amongst first-generation Asian migrants the shared experiences of migration and settlement in a hostile environment provided sufficient impetus to forge strong bonds of support (Mattausch, 1998). However, over a decade ago writers began to argue that the momentum generating ethnic cohesion would slowly dissipate and the resources enabling Asian businesses to develop a competitive advantage would evaporate as successive generations achieved greater social and economic integration (Parekh, 1989). Modood (1992) reinforced this view by arguing that the value ascribed to the social capital of ethnic members would outgrow the resources available within the boundaries of their ethnic collective: 'Like the Jews before them, the Indian family and kinship networks will last as long as Indians are not able to flourish without them' (p. 43).

Second-generation Asian migrants

The focus of attention on social capital within the Asian community now turns to the younger generation, who, as expected, have achieved considerable integration (although this does vary across the different religious sub-groups). A number of writers describe the experiences of the younger generation of British Asians as adopting a 'dual existence', negotiating the transition between traditional cultural values and the dominant 'youth culture' (Harper, 1982; Watson, 1984). Rather than a direct decline in the reliance on embedded networks within ethnic groups as forecast by Modood (1992), younger British Asians have developed a far more complex relationship both with their ethnic community and with wider groups they choose to participate in. 'Cruisers' (Janjuha-Jivraj and Dickson, 1999) described the younger generation of British Asians who are able to navigate their way between the 'conflicting' environments as part of their daily existence. This group of young British Asians has experienced a shift in their exchanges with the ethnic community, and simultaneously achieved greater confidence through increased interactions with groups whose membership was perhaps unattainable to the same extent for their parents.

The new generation of Asian businesses are evolving, moving away from the traditional moulds initially established to provide a base for generating stability, 'breaking-out' (Ram and Hillin, 1994) from traditional ethnic markets. Zhou (1998) argues that a combination of factors needs to be considered when researching ethnic businesses. These include personal networks of the individual and their cultural identity – the social capital of entrepreneurs, and also the industrial sector of the business. The choice of business industry is important to note as it often represents the degree of integration achieved by ethnic groups. Businesses that have moved out of ethnic-specific markets represent a greater degree of integration and the potential for longer-term survival. Ram and

Smallbone (2001), however, highlight a number of reports that continue to record low take-up of formalised financial support amongst ethnic businesses (Bank of England, 1999):

> whilst there is little documented evidence of EMBs [Ethnic Minority Businesses] suffering discrimination by finance providers in the UK, there is evidence that some EMBs perceive they are treated adversely ... and perception may be more important than reality in this context. (Bank of England, 1999, p. 35, cited in Ram and Smallbone, 2001)

The concerns stated in the Bank of England report should not be underestimated: if the younger generation feel they do not receive required support or are unlikely to be treated as favourably as their white counterparts, the wider effectiveness of embedded networks diminishes. Hence Bachkaniwala *et al.* (2001) argue that there is a pervasive need for continued informal sources of financial support through embedded networks of ethnic entrepreneurs. However, a further source of confusion within this perspective originates from the often overlooked heterogeneity of the Asian business community (Janjuha-Jivraj and Woods, 2002). The various sub-groups display differing levels of socio-economic integration through factors such as educational-attainment nature of employment, unemployment levels and even spatial distribution for both housing and work. To address the deficiency offered by business support providers, ethnic communities rely on the motivation of donors to offer support through the networks, once again reinforcing and maintaining the distinct forms of cultural capital. The degree of sophistication amongst the informal services offered within an ethnic community is often a reflection of the sophistication of members' businesses as they progress along their life-cycles.

As migrant family businesses evolve over the successive generations, their reliance on resources experiences significant transition. The nature of social capital changes considerably as the younger generation becomes more integrated with the mainstream and perhaps less reliant on ethnic resources. Researchers exploring social capital argue that greater integration of the younger generation inevitably leads to the demise of the ethnic networks of migrant communities (Modood, 1992). In order to explore this phenomenon, the following questions are addressed in this chapter:

- Why does the informal form of exchange persist within communities?
- What forms of social capital are evident and how important are they in sustaining relationships within the religious-ethnic community?
- How crucial is the community in providing an infrastructure within which support can be offered?

Methodology

Whilst studies based in a geographical location will often focus on a particular sub-group with a notable presence, more often than not the distinction between various sub-groups in terms of economic development is overlooked. Modood and Berthoud (1997) initiated a more comprehensive approach to understanding the British Asian community. They argued that acknowledging the varying levels of economic and educational achievements amongst the sub-groups enabled richer and more beneficial analysis to be generated. This research draws upon the experiences of two sub-groups within the British Asian community, the Ismaili Muslim community and the Vanik Hindu community. Many members of both groups shared experiences of double migration (Indian subcontinent to the United Kingdom via East Africa – Kenya, Uganda, Tanzania). As a whole, these communities are described as highly entrepreneurial with strong cultures of social capital.

The research in this chapter adopts the grounded theory approach (Strauss and Corbin, 1990) in order to explore relationships with embedded networks, as this area is still in its exploratory stages. By adopting this method the discussion has explored a range of issues and developed ideas for further research. The data in this chapter is based on twelve cases consisting of in-depth semi-structured interviews with both generations (typically father and son) actively involved in the business. Criteria stipulated for the generation of a sample stated that the cases needed to be members of either of the above two sub-groups, family firms (defined as a business with two generations actively involved on a daily basis), and based within Greater London (in order to limit the geographical range of the network). Potential respondents were identified through community leaders, and snowballing techniques enabled subsequent cases to be generated. The very specific nature of the sample generated through the strict criteria meant that snowballing techniques were felt to be sufficient in order to generate a range of businesses that would present a representative sample of both sub-groups. Interviews were conducted with both generations separately through face-to-face interactions (all interviews were tape-recorded and transcribed). Wherever possible, the interviews were conducted with each respondent in the same organisation in rapid succession. There was no cross-referencing between respondents in the same case. Table 5.1 presents a brief profile of the respondents and the businesses. For clarity the older respondents in each case were assigned 'A' after their case number and the younger respondents were classified with 'B' after their case number.

Table 5.1 Summary of participating firms

Case	*Family involvment*	*Industry classification*	*Customer base*
1	Father and Daughter	Commercial sales and letting	B2C (non-ethnic specific)
2	Father and Son	Import/export	B2B (non-ethnic specific)
3	Father and Son	Import/export	B2B (non-ethnic specific)
4	Father and Son	Clothing manufacture and trading	B2B (non-ethnic specific)
5	Father and Son	Fast-food catering and outlets	B2C (non-ethnic specific)
6	Father and Daughter	Distribution of agricultural products	B2B (non-ethnic specific)
7	Father and Son	Property and leisure investment	B2C (non-ethnic specific)
8	Father and Son	Processing dry Asian ingredients	B2B (ethnic and non-ethnic)
9	Mother and Son	Catering and retail outlet	B2C (non-ethnic specific)
10	Father and Son	Distrib. of confectionary products	B2B (non-ethnic specific)
11	Father and Son	Chain of hotels	B2C (non-ethnic specific)
12	Father and Son	Chain of hotels and restaurants	B2C (non-ethnic specific)

B2B = Business to Business
B2C = Business to Consumer

The interviews explored how respondents perceived their involvement in business support networks. This consisted of an analysis of their participation within their own ethnic networks as well as external sources of business support. The qualitative nature of the interviews enabled respondents to describe their involvement with these different systems in their own words as fully as possible. Where respondents described involvement with external business support agencies they were asked to give examples of the type of programmes they were participating in. Common examples included local Chambers of Commerce, Federation of Small Businesses and trade associations. By not specifying the nature of external business support this enabled the respondents to self-determine what they considered as business support. The same approach was also adopted for involvement with their ethnic community (from both a business and social perspective). The distinction between business and social involvement was an important means of generating a greater understanding of the nature of their participation within the ethnic community. Ethnic networks as a base of business support also provided a means by which respondents included personal contacts. This was predominantly the case for the older respondents, as the ethnic networks provided most if not all of their business and social contacts. The younger respondents were asked specific questions about contacts generated through university or their professions prior to joining the business.

The following tables present the responses of both generations. The responses were categorised in the following classifications based on the data generated from the respondents. The contents of the tables include quotes from the respondents as they described their interaction with external and ethnic networks.

Findings and discussion

Tables 5.2 and 5.3 represent respondent involvement in their embedded networks. The following categories were highlighted as important for this research:

- *Active* – self-assessment of involvement without specifying the direct nature of their interaction, encompassing Hite's (2000) various levels of personal, dyadic and social capital. 
- *Information* – self-perception of the degree of reliance on the ethnic community for business-related information. Interaction may be through formalised business-related seminars within the community or through interpersonal networks. 

Table 5.2 Involvement in the ethnic community network (older generation)

Case	*Active*	*Information*	*Contacts*	*Social/religious*
1A	No	No	No	No
2A	Yes	Yes	Yes – business partners	Yes – a lot
3A	Yes	Very little usage	Limited	Yes
4A	Yes	Sometimes	No, too specialised	Yes
5A	Yes	Not really	Some contacts useful	Yes
6A	Yes	Not really	No, too specialised	Yes
7A	No	Not really	Not at all	Not active
8A	Yes	Never considered	Not really	Yes
9A	Yes	Yes	No need	Yes
10A	Yes	Not really	No	Yes
11A	No	Previously	No	Previously
12A	Yes	Not really	Not much help	Yes

Table 5.3 Involvement in the ethnic community network (younger generation)

Case	*Active*	*Information*	*Contacts*	*Social/religious*
1B	No	No	No	No
2B	Yes	No	Yes – business partners	Yes
3B	Yes	Yes	Yes	Yes
4B	Yes	Yes	No	Yes
5B	Yes	No	No	Yes
6B	Yes	No	No	Yes
7B	Yes and No	Limited	Not any more	No
8B	Yes	No	Yes, a little	Yes
9B	Not really	No	No	No
10B	Yes	No	No	Yes
11B	No	No	No	Limited
12B	Yes and No	No	No	Little

- *Contacts* – generated from the ethnic network, involving various aspects of resource accessibility (Hite, 2000), including recruitment and/or business generated from community members as well as access to external third parties.
- *Social* – a broad range of relationships, covering the three main aspects of personal relationships (Hite, 2000) and the religious dimension of the ethnic community.

Experiences of the older generation

The degree of interaction with the ethnic community varied amongst the older respondents (Table 5.2), with greater emphasis on social aspects of the community. Social participation seemed to be a key determinant for respondents in deciding their involvement with the community, more so than business-based exchanges. When discussing business relationships some respondents were quite ambiguous about their interactions: for example, 11A had separated from his religious group completely, although other family members still participated in social and religious customs. 11A maintained he did not draw upon his ethnic contacts for business purposes, yet it was later discovered he had a formal business partnership with respondent 1A (who was from the same community). Rather than acknowledge this collaboration 11A presented an image of a powerful independent presence without the need for embedded networks. Although the experiences of 11A were the exception, a number of older respondents felt their relationships with ethnic networks had decreased considerably over time. The initial support structures generated from this strong solidarity had encouraged business patronage on the basis of a shared ethnic identity. As businesses had developed, however, and families and communities achieved greater degrees of economic and social stability, this need for group-based support had diminished: 'When we first came and had the shops, Indians would go out of their way to help each other and do business with you. Now they don't care, that has gone' (10A). Respondent 10A cited examples where the family had withdrawn business involvement from the community because of discord amongst fellow members. Other respondents gave examples of community-based collaborations that had not been successful, forcing them to break these links and focus on developing the business relying exclusively on the family's resources: 'In the past we worked with people from within the community, but it was not very effective. Now we prefer to work within the family' (3A).

The relationship between the older generation and the religious ethnic community across most of the cases followed a similar complex pattern. Older respondents described their involvement with the community on a social level, but when considering business support answers were more varied. This discussion has highlighted some of the negative experiences of working within the parameters of the community, but for many a strong sense of loyalty meant it was difficult to criticise the resources offered when they did not fulfil business needs. 9A was the only respondent who openly felt the community was crucial to her business, as it provided an important customer base.

Whilst there was an ambiguity about business support, many older respondents were very positive about the social benefits derived from the community. Respondents shared examples of where their relationship with the ethnic community was a two-way process, thus building on the social capital of the community: '[I am involved with] a lot of voluntary help with various committees . . [it] is very important and I enjoy being involved with the community' (9A). The impact of this distinction between drawing on social rather than business support presents a shift in the perceived social capital embedded within the community. This is an important consideration as the next generation looks to balance the resources available and the urgency for economic integration reduces. Is the emphasis on support from the community more likely to be in the form of cultural capital rather than social capital?

New beginnings or reinventing the wheel? The younger generation

The responses of the younger generation in Table 5.3 are far clearer compared with those given by their parents (Table 5.2). This is particularly evident as the younger generation are more objective about their interactions with the community. Where the younger generation felt they did not have an exchange with the community according to the various categories, they were more willing to be direct about their lack of involvement.

The younger generation did not exhibit the same degree of emotional attachment towards the community as did their parents. This was likely to be the result of a lack of shared intense emotions such as those generated via migration. This emotional detachment manifested itself as the younger generation consciously seemed to implement a clear distinction between their reliance on business and social resources from the community: 'The business group is good for networking. I try to avoid taking advice from the community because I find it compromises positions and relationships' (8B).

The lack of involvement amongst the older generation was an influential factor determining the degree of interaction of the younger generation. This was illustrated in cases where neither generation had involvement with the community (1B and 11B). 11B replicated the pattern displayed by his father by not acknowledging the business partnerships sourced from the community, whilst 1B attributed her lack of involvement with the community as a family trait: 'Not really, my parents aren't involved in the community at all and neither are we' (1B).

Where the younger generation felt they were actively involved in the community there were some notable differences between their perceptions and levels of involvement compared with the older generation. This is likely to stem from different expectations of involvement. The literature review considered various approaches to social capital, highlighting work by Portes (1998), who emphasised the importance of trust and direct or indirect reciprocity. The factors influencing group cohesion have inevitably declined in intensity as the external factors facing group members progressively became less harsh and the ethnic population achieved a degree of integration. As a result, the form of community interaction and, more importantly, nature of social capital available also change, and what the younger generation considers to be involvement may be very superficial for the older generation who experienced the strong sense of cohesion upon migration.

The younger generation exhibits the impact of mixed embedded networks (Kloosterman *et al.*, 1999) as they balance the benefits they derive from members of multiple groups rather than focusing predominantly on their ethnic community for both business and social needs. Table 5.4 presents a profile of the cases and their relationships with external support agencies. The data in this table are based on agencies

Table 5.4 Use of external support services (younger generation)

Case	*Member**	*Ind req***	*Other info. sources*	*Comments*
1B	Yes – both	Yes	Colleagues	Father proactive
2B	Yes – both	N/A	No one else	Son proactive
3B	Yes – both	N/A	Colleagues	Son proactive
4B	Yes – both	N/A	No one	Son proactive
5B	No	N/A	No one else	Father proactive
6B	No – both	N/A	Bus. advisors	Difference in use of services
7B	No – both	N/A	No one	Neither
8B	Yes – both	N/A	Trade org.	Son proactive
9B	No – both	N/A	Bank – finance only	Neither – both same attitudes
10B	No – both	N/A	Bank adequate	Son proactive
11B	No – both	N/A	Internal team	Father proactive
12B	Yes – both	N/A	Lawyers, accountants	Father proactive

* Membership of professional organisation.
** Ind Req: Industry Requirement to join professional organisation.

identified by the respondents during the course of the interview. As was the case with ethnic embedded networks, the generations in each case displayed broadly similar attitudes towards reliance on external support agencies.

However, the surprising finding in this section was the almost equal split between the activity of fathers and sons towards external support. This illustrates that the embedded networks of the older generation were wider than perhaps initially expected. With the exception of Case 1, none of the businesses needed membership of an industry organisation to operate. The types of organisations to which respondents belonged varied from industry support networks to general management organisations. The cases that did not interact with external organisations relied on informal sources of support, predominantly in the form of advice from associated professionals – bank managers, lawyers or accountants. Reliance on these relationships meant these respondents did not feel the need to develop other relationships. Case 11 had a well-developed form of business assistance by internalising the sources of business support through employing in-house advisors. 11B had also delegated his networking by using these individuals to attend trade events and meetings to gather information and build up the contact base for the business. Hence, rather than relying on the personal network of the founder as an individual, relationships were developed with the business as a whole. Where an individual relationship was based on trust, the notion of reciprocity building a relationship with the business as a single unit made this much more difficult. Individual trust and goodwill were still paramount, but the emphasis had shifted to the business as a unit rather than the individual entrepreneur. However, this approach still incorporated the attributes of the founder into the wider culture of the business. Typical entrepreneurial literature emphasises the centrality of the founder in the networks relating to the business. As highlighted, the approach adopted in Case 11 bucks this trend.

Conclusion

The findings in this chapter have illustrated various forms of embedded networks across both generations. The older migrant community provided a strong base of social capital that individuals and families were able to utilise to develop their financial and social base and in turn fulfil their obligations by offering support through chain migration. In the literature review considerable emphasis was placed on the ethnic community providing support, and also protection from the racism of wider society. However Table 5.4 highlights the involvement of the older generation with external organisations. This may have been the result of either the ethnic community not fulfilling business needs or a conscious decision for individuals to expand their embedded networks.

Contrary to predictions of writers such as Modood (1992) and Parekh (1989), involvement with the ethnic community has not diminished amongst the younger generation. Instead, the findings illustrate that the younger generation have developed wider embedded networks and shifted their use of the various communities they belong to, thus displaying greater comfort with wider multicultural groups. The integration they achieved through socialisation during education and wider working experiences has enabled the younger generation to develop greater confidence both socially and for business. Furthermore, wider societal changes have also enabled the migrant communities to carve out their niche in a more tolerant and welcoming society. These cases are good examples of how reliance on ethnic communities has evolved over generations. Where the community was initially a strong source of protection and support and even generated business opportunities for the older generation, the younger generation can objectively decide whether the ethnic community is the right source for business support. Whilst they do not rely heavily on the ethnic community for business support, the younger generation in this group still placed considerable importance on the community for social, religious and identity needs.

Attitudes towards ethnic embedded networks would have been quite different if the cases had an ethnic-specific customer base. However the businesses involved in this research had a wide customer base and did not occupy typical niches associated with ethnic-specific markets. It would be interesting to conduct a comparative piece of work with businesses targeted almost exclusively to an Asian customer base. The responses of both generations showed it was reasonable to assert that for most of the cases external support agencies provided information and access to wider markets. Although ethnic communities offered similar services, the emphasis amongst these respondents was on developing links with the wider community in order to broaden their personal embedded networks. As discussed in the previous section, the external relationships were generated primarily by the younger generation, and the importance of these networks were recognised by the older generation.

On the whole, the older generation conveyed a deeper sense of loyalty and commitment to the ethnic community and was less keen to be critical of its business resources. The younger generation, on the other hand, was more objective and exhibited fewer emotional attachments that influenced their reflections on the community. Various factors are cited as influencing the changing nature of the relationship between business and ethnic networks. As the younger generation become more integrated with society their need to rely on the community decreases. Work by Portes (1998) emphasised the influence of the community through enforcing members to conform to the implicit rules. These rules helped to maintain the spirit of social capital as community members settle, and their acceptance of help is reciprocated through support to successive migrants. However, the impact of the community can also be constraining, as individuals identify that opportunities for further development, expansion or diversification are not without risk. Durkheim (1984, cited in Portes, 1998) emphasised the importance of status within society amongst migrant groups by highlighting it as a means of repayment for providing support. Ambitious business ventures and taking risky decisions can lead to failure, which in turn could result in a loss of status, for both the individual and the family within their embedded network. Case 11B was the only business that was preparing to float the business and had experienced very rapid expansion. If the founder is not actively involved in the ethnic community, it is unlikely that members will have awareness of business activities and this means they will have limited information about failures. This then means that the founder can generate an image of success, without community members being aware of other support structures or previous failed attempts. Such behaviour helps to propagate the image of the founder with the Midas touch. This also makes it very difficult for subsequent generations to take over the business and live up to the image created by the founder.

The relationship between the younger generation and the ethnic community is a complex process rather than, as expected, a straightforward decline. Although the younger generation consciously reduced their involvement with the ethnic community for business purposes, they still considered the community as an important source from which they derived their identity and fulfilled certain social needs. In addition, they also expressed the desire to give something back to the community. The sense of obligation in providing support to members was ingrained in a number of younger respondents and they felt they were in a position to support the community. In certain cases this meant providing the same types of business support and advice, initially offered to their parents, to the new waves of community migrants who were experiencing similar challenges and barriers to business start-up to those experienced by migrants during the 1970s.

One can conclude that the reliance on ethnic communities by Asian family firms has indeed changed as a result of broadening embedded ethnic networks. This is inevitable having analysed the impact of socialisation and integration of the younger generation. However, the surprising aspect is the continued value placed on maintaining the cultural capital of the embedded ethnic networks. This was exemplified by the younger generation respondents assuming responsibility in acting as donors to provide support to successive co-ethnic migrants. The distinction, however, between this form of exchange and that experienced by their parents is the context within which this exchange occurs. Previously social capital available to ethnic migrants crossed the boundaries based on religious group affiliation, as discussed earlier. The factors motivating solidarity were strong enough to generate a close form of group cooperation and support. As these families and sub-groups achieved economic and social stability and with that a greater degree of integration, the need for wide solidarity diminished. When the younger generation described group affiliation, it was broadly split between wider non-ethnic-specific organisations or peer groups and their own religious-ethnic community. The support they donated was offered solely to their own religious-ethnic community, and this was the main, sometimes only ethnic-specific, group they considered to be part of their embedded networks.

Reciprocity and the nature of debt within cultural capital continue to be important influences for the next generation of members belonging to these community groups. This has manifested itself through their willingness to offer support within their community. When one considers the nature of embedded networks of the younger generation, it is not sufficient to describe this as a combination of resources from their ethnic networks and the results of their personal integration. An argument in the literature review stated that the embedded networks of first-generation Asian migrants were limited by the confines of the community due to the lack of community integration. The parameters of the embedded networks for the younger generation have expanded to such an extent that the distinction between the ethnic group and wider community is likely to be very blurred. As these barriers start to fall, the compartments of each group fulfilling specific economic and or social needs also decline. This leads to an embedded network where it becomes almost impossible to identify which segments support various aspects of the individual's life. Therefore it becomes difficult to predict *when* the importance placed on ethnic communities will diminish. Instead, the question we need to ask is how future support will be offered and, more important, what the nature of that support will be.

Notes

1. This chapter was first published as the following article: S. Janjuha-Jivraj, 'The Sustainability of Social Capital within Ethnic Networks', *Journal of Business Ethics*, 47(1), (2003), 31–43. With kind permission from Kluwer Academic Publishers.
2. The term 'Asian' refers to individuals who originate from the Indian subcontinent, either directly or via East Africa.

References

Adler, P. and S.-W. Kwon, 'Social Capital: Prospects for a New Concept', *Academy of Management Review*, 27(1), (2002) 17–40.

Bachkaniwala, D., M. Wright and M. Ram, 'Succession in South Asian Family Businesses in the UK', *International Small Business Journal*, 19(4), (2001) 15–27.

Ballard, R. and C. Hurst (eds), *Desh Pardesh: The South Asian Presence in Britain* (London: Hurst Publishers, 1994).

Blackburn, R., A. Dale and J. Jarman, 'Ethnic Differences in Attainment in Education, Occupation and Life-style', in V. Karn (ed.), *Ethnicity in the 1991 Census, Volume 4, Employment, Education and Housing Among the Ethnic Minority Populations of Britain* (London: Office for National Statistics, 1997), pp. 242–64.

Brehm, J. and W. Rahn, 'Individuals-Level Evidence for the Causes and Consequences of Social Capital', *American Journal of Political Science*, 41(3), (1997) 999–1023.

Desai, R., *Indian Immigrants in Britain*, Institute of Race Relations (Oxford: Oxford University Press, 1963).

Fadahunsi, A., D. Smallbone and S. Supri, 'Networking and Ethnic Minority Enterprise Development: Insights from a North London Study', *Small Business and Enterprise Development*, 7(3), (2000) 228–40.

Harper, R., 'Some Sociological Considerations', in UNESCO Press, *Living in Two Cultures* (London: Gower Publishing, 1982).

Hiro, D., *Black British, White British – A History of Race Relations in Britain* (London: Grafton Books, 1991).

Hite, J., 'Qualities of Embedded Network Ties of Emerging Entrepreneurial Firms', *Frontiers of Entrepreneurial Research* (Babson Kauffman Foundation Conference Proceedings, 2000) accessed at www.babson.edu/entrep/fer/IV/IVC/IVC.htm.

Janjuha-Jivraj, S. and K. Dickson, 'Transitional Challenges within South Asian Family Businesses', Paper presented at the Small Business and Enterprise Development Conference (Leeds University, 1999).

Janjuha-Jivraj, S. and A. Woods, 'Successional Issues within Asian Family Firms: Learning from the Kenyan Experience', *International Small Business Journal*, 20(1), (2002) 77–94.

Kloosterman, R., J. Van der Leun and J. Rath, 'Mixed Embeddedness: (In)formal Economic Activity and Immigrant Businesses in the Netherlands', *International Journal of Urban Regional Research*, 23(2), (1999) 252.

Lyon, M., 'Ethnicity in Britain: The Gujurati Tradition', *New Community* (1971–3) 1–2, 121–41.

Marger, M., 'Social and Human Capital in Immigrant Adaptation: The Case of Canadian Business Immigrants', *The Journal of Social Economics*, 30(2), (2001) 169.

Mattausch, J., 'From Subjects to Citizens: British East African Asians', *Journal of Ethnic and Migratory Studies*, 24(1), (1998) 121–41.

Modood, T., *Not Easy Being British: Colour and Citizenship* (Runnymede Trust and Trentham Books, Stoke on Trent, 1992).

Modood, T. and R. Berthoud, *Ethnic Minorities in Britain: Diversity and Disadvantage* (London: Policy Studies Institute, 1997).

Parekh, B., *Britain: A Plural Society* Seminar Report, Discussion Paper No.3 (London: Commission for Racial Equality, 1989).

Portes, A. 'Social Capital: Its Origins and Applications in Modern Sociology', *Annual Review of Sociology*, 24, (1998) 1–24.

Ram, M., *Managing to Survive – Working lives in Small Firms* (Oxford: Blackwell Business, 1994a).

Ram, M., 'Unravelling Social Networks in Ethnic Minority Firms', *International Small Business Journal*, 12(3) (1994b) 42–54.

Ram, M. and G. Hillin, 'Achieving 'Break-out' Developing Mainstream Ethnic Minority Businesses', *Small Business and Enterprise Development*, 1, (1994) 15–21.

Ram, M. and D. Smallbone, *Ethnic Minority Enterprise: Policy in Practice* (Report prepared for the Small Business Service, 2001).

Srinivasan, S., 'The Class Position of the Asian Petty Bourgeoisie', *New Community*, 19(1), (1992) 61–74.

Strauss, A. and J. Corbin, *Basics of Qualitative Research* (London: Sage Publications, 1990).

Watson, J. (ed.), *Between Two Cultures: Migrants and Minorities in Britain* (Oxford: Basil Blackwell, 1984).

Werbner, P., 'Renewing an Industrial Past: British Pakistani Entrepreneurship in Manchester', *Migration*, 8, (1990) 17–41.

Zhou, Y., 'Beyond Ethnic Enclaves: Location Strategies of Chinese Producer Service Firms in Los Angeles', *Economic Geography*, 74(3), (1998) 228–52.

6

Engaging SMEs in Community and Social Issues

Clare Southwell[1]

The need to promote socially responsible business practice among small and medium sized businesses in the United Kingdom (UK) was identified as a priority by Dr Kim Howells, then Minister for Corporate Social Responsibility, in the government's 'Business and Society' report in March 2001. Recent research suggests that SMEs in the UK may make a social contribution worth up to £3bn each year – about ten times that of large corporations. As SMEs are important to a range of economic and social initiatives in the UK and Europe, increasing the quality and extent of SME contributions to such initiatives is seen as vital to promoting the overall positive impact of businesses.

A range of organisations from the public and not-for-profit sectors, including those who have contributed to the research reported on in this chapter, have an interest in promoting responsible business practice. It is envisaged that these organisations should work together, where possible, to develop and promote a common agenda to achieve this goal.

The research project 'Engaging SMEs in Community & Social Issues' was a consortium research study on behalf of the Department of Trade and Industry, led by Business in the Community, with the British Chambers of Commerce, the Institute of Directors and AccountAbility (the Institute of Social and Ethical Accountability) (2002). The research aim was better to understand, with a view to increasing, the engagement of SMEs in responsible business practice. This chapter covers the role of relationships and values in SMEs developing typologies of owner-managers, terminology relating to community, environmental and social activities, current practice, motivations and barriers to engagement and finally how to engage SMEs further.

An initial research framework was produced on the basis of desk research to ascertain precious lessons learned about engaging SMEs, policy interviews with SME specialist organisations and SMEs, consultation with members of a reference group, drawn from practitioners and SMEs, and best-practice learning from other organisations engaging with SMEs. These are referred to in the text, with some of the publications used referenced at the end. Since this was not a full academic research project, specific citations are limited.

The qualitative and quantitative primary research among SMEs themselves was undertaken among 200 Managing Directors of SMEs and through five group discussions across the country. For the purposes of this project, we used the DTI and EU guidelines (2001), which define small and medium enterprises as organisations with under 250 employees, turnover of under 40 million Euros (£27 million), and over 25 per cent owner-managed (see Appendix A.1).

The role of relationships and values in SMEs

Throughout the project a common theme emerging from the research is that SMEs and the nature of their relationships with key stakeholders need to be differentiated from each other, if the business case, motivations and barriers and current patterns of responsible business practice are to be fully understood. The Forum of Private Business (2002) has developed the concept of the 'small business ethos', defining SMEs in terms of developmental stages achieved in key relationships, such as:

- *Employer/employee relationships* (e.g. selection, recruitment, terms and conditions, training, definition of responsibilities, career path substitutions).
- *Business/bank relationships* (e.g. financing, understanding and application of risk assessment, alternative funding, asset management).
- *Customer/supplier relationships* (e.g. differences in formal and informal quality control processes, informal understandings within supply chains, marketing, selling, PR).
- *Business/regulatory enforcement* (e.g. how compliance with 'red tape' is achieved, relationship with enforcement officials).

From start-up to maturity, these SME relationships evolve through different stages, although it is not suggested that all SMEs develop along a common path. The Forum of Private Business (FPB) also stressed that the relationships between SMEs and their key stakeholders – notably employers and customers – are qualitatively different from those of large businesses, characterised by a high level of informality. Customer relationships are often based on personal knowledge of the customer's needs, while employee relationships are more family-like, with greater cordiality and social integration.

Such relationships, by virtue of their more intimate nature, are seen as inherently more 'responsible' than the more impersonal relationships associated with big businesses. Therefore, a small business may consider itself to be a 'responsible business', even though it may not be formally recognised. This is reinforced by this research project, which shows that 96 per cent of SMEs feel they have responsible business practices.

A somewhat different, although related, conception of SME development has been put forward by David Grayson, BITC director and Principal of the new virtual corporate university for Small Business Service Business Links, and David Irwin, then director of the Small Business Service. In a November 2001 Royal Society for the encouragement of Arts, Manufacture and Commerce lecture, they proposed that businesses progress through distinct stages of relationships with support networks as they develop:

- *'Just do it.'* Entrepreneurs at this stage are characterised by self-belief and a tendency to overestimate the likelihood of success. These entrepreneurs attempt to act as independently as possible. They focus on attracting resources and persuading others to believe in them, with a minimum of support or advice from others.
- *Flying solo*. Once they are fully in business, these entrepreneurs are proud of what they have achieved but some are also too embarrassed about what they still do not know to seek advice from others. The most successful entrepreneurs generally recognise their shortcomings and address them.
- *Support seekers*. These individuals are starting to think strategically and are undertaking key tasks for the first time, such as employing people, exporting, introducing total quality management or raising equity. Those who recognise they need support for these activities are far more likely to be successful in the long run.
- *Active networking*. The pinnacle is recognition by the entrepreneur that support and advice is essential to business growth and does not need to come solely from professional advisers but can come from a myriad of sources. The most effective entrepreneurs are those who network voraciously.

Allied to relationships are values, particularly those of SME owner-managers. Understanding the owner-manager's perceived purpose of the business and their motivations for running it may provide useful guidance in developing the business case and tools for promoting responsible business practice.

With this in mind, the primary research element of this project also focused on motivations for starting up and running a small or medium sized organisation. One of the most important aspects of running an SME was seen to be (as well as 'to earn a decent living') independence and a greater sense of personal fulfilment and by being in control. This personal aspect is a strong dictator of the motivators and the actual involvement of SMEs in community and social initiatives.

The 'types' identified through our research process are outlined below. Support for and encouragement in promoting the responsible business practices will need to be different for each of these distinct groups:

- *'Ben & Anitas'* (Referring to 'Ben and Jerry's' and Anita Roddick of the Body Shop): SMEs which have been started as 'social enterprises', in which the owner/managers are motivated heavily by a desire to create a positive community or social impact. These organisations are more likely to understand Corporate Social Responsibility (CSR) concepts and jargon and seek out information and opportunities for engagement.
- *Arthur Daleys* (Refers to a financially motivated fictional character in a UK television programme): These are motivated purely by financial gain, seeing no relevance for social engagement, and are unlikely to be active members of business networks. They believe they have no social responsibilities outside the narrow confines of their business.
- *One-offs*: These are individuals who have had relatively minimal experience of engagement with the social responsibility agenda. They may have participated in a volunteering project, for example. Once engaged, they could progress to become another 'type', depending on their underlying motivations and circumstances. Motivations tend to be issue-based.
- *DIYers* (Do it Yourself): These fiercely independent individuals work in isolation from others
- *Smart pragmatists*: These individuals recognise the business benefits of acting responsibly – e.g. big business customers demanding evidence of good environmental practices as a condition of winning contracts. However, the motives of these individuals differ from those of enlightened pragmatists, who are motivated by broader, long-term societal goals and understand the basic business case. This latter type would be motivated to improve their environmental practices by

a desire to improve the environment generally and run a sustainable business.

The different underlying motivations and experiences of these groups mean that:

- The motivations and business case will differ across these groups. A DIYer, for example, will not be as motivated by opportunities to achieve Public Relations profile as much as the pragmatists and therefore the business case should be presented differently for each of them.
- Language needs to be tailored for each of the groups. In promoting responsible business practice, communication with one-offs, who have had less experience of engagement, needs to be simpler and more concrete than with 'Ben & Anitas', who are likely to be more familiar with CSR jargon.
- Types of support required will differ across groups. One-offs will need to be educated about the business case for engagement to a greater extent than enlightened pragmatists, who will be familiar with the business case and need more practical guidance for improving the quality of their activities.

At a strategic level, government and third-party organisations interested in promoting SME engagement with CSR can direct their resources more cost-effectively to maximise engagement across the universe of SMEs. They might, for example, decide to focus initially on smart and enlightened pragmatists and not attempt to engage Arthur Daleys. The 'Ben & Anitas' could be used as a network of role models to 'sell' CSR to other groups. A map of these types is shown in Figure 6.1. This is not intended to be comprehensive or to scale but rather a starting point for further action and research.

Terminology

There is universal agreement that 'corporate social responsibility' is not the most useful, or indeed effective, phrase to describe the spectrum of community, environmental and social activities SMEs undertake. In each of the group discussions, the issue of terminology came up spontaneously in the first few minutes.

Although 'corporate social responsibility' was the most common phrase used (spontaneously by 28 per cent in the quantitative research), this

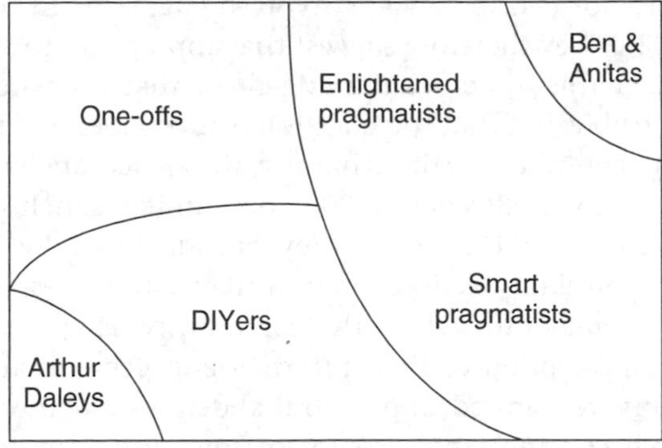

Figure 6.1 Proposed SME typologies

is seen to be driven by the need to build relationships with key audiences, particularly large-business customers and government. CSR was also seen in discussions as a barrier to further involvement as it evoked the spectre of regulation, perceived as burdensome to SMEs. 'Corporate social responsibility' was also seen as an abstract term and there was a strong desire for concrete language, using terms from everyday life, e.g. 'recycling' or 'energy cost reduction'.

'Responsible business practice' was used by 17 per cent in the quantitative research, but SMEs tend to feel this is something different or more mainstream than CSR. 'Community involvement' is also cited by one in eight but is often seen by SMEs as restrictive.

Suggestions for improving terminology to describe responsible business practice included:

- emphasising the totality of responsible business practice
- using simple action verbs which focus on the relationship or interaction a business has with the community and environment, or how a business helps the community
- emphasising the pragmatic value to the business
- being careful not to be exclusive
- avoiding the prospect of additional regulation, bureaucracy or impositions

Current practice

It is clear that SMEs' social and community activities are fragmented and informal. The Federation of Small Businesses also suggests that many SMEs do not realise they are involved (Department of Trade and Industry, 2002). They therefore suggest that approaches to SMEs should be couched in terms of an acknowledgement that they are by default socially responsible, but that the question is to what extent they 'go the extra mile' and contribute to the economy, workplace, and environment. The Forum of Private Business (2002) has similar conclusions – that many businesses would consider they are already fully engaged in Corporate Responsibility action through their employees and through the service they may provide for the community. However, in reality, this may be a perception of their informal engagement, and may not equate with any 'recognised' approach that defines CSR more formally.

This research confirms this – 'A lot of companies are doing it, and do not know they are doing it' was a popular comment in our group discussions (and enforced by the hard data). Many SMEs see community and social activity as an 'add on', rather than an integral part of mainstream business. It tends to be those most engaged and those realising hard business benefits who view CSR initiatives as part of their organisation. This contrasts with environmental and employment issues which tend not to be viewed under the CSR umbrella, and are more likely to be seen as integral.

In addition, it is clear that many organisations do not have a formal social or environmental policy. In fact, Mazars Neville Russell research (2001) claims that only one in six SMEs have any policy relating to community or social activity. Again, this should not be taken as an indication that companies are not concerned, as our research shows that 84 per cent of SMEs say they have discussed these issues internally in the last year.

A number of organisations do approach these activities more formally – or understand their fit with the business – if their organisation meets or adheres to business quality models. However, this research shows that 67 per cent of SMEs do not use any business models or quality standards, and that one in six has Investors in People, and a further one in six has an ISO (International Standards Organisation) standard.

The most popular social responsibility activity among SMEs is internal, with over four in five SMEs saying they encourage skill development, encourage work/life balance and take responsibility for the health and wellbeing of staff. The internal aspect is perhaps the most distinctive feature of SME involvement, and is a difference from the larger businesses who tend to be motivated by external pressures. Staff are often the motivation, the catalyst and the focus of the activity and communication, and are also seen as the key beneficiaries. Environmental activity is also high, with two in three actively reducing their environmental impact, recycling or reducing waste.

Community involvement (often seen as the main factor under the term of CSR) is also high. Sixty per cent work with local schools or colleges (educational links and skills/training being most mentioned in discussions), and 52 per cent work with charities or the voluntary sector, although only 53 per cent would say they were active in the local community.

Overall, there is a high correlation between importance placed on and involvement with activities. However, the biggest gaps between importance placed and actual involvement are social exclusion and ethical sourcing (33 per cent and 54 per cent respectively believe these to be important for SMEs, but only 16 per cent and 31 per cent are actually involved).

The group discussions showed a real diversity in communication – some communicated to large business customers because they had to, but the key communication was to employees. The quantitative research showed there is a lot of communication with employees (89 per cent do), but it drops dramatically for external audiences, although over half of those with external shareholders do communicate to that audience as well. After that, SMEs are most likely to involve and inform customers and suppliers, with only 30 per cent saying they have communicated at all with either government (central or local) or the media (trade, local or national).

Motivations and barriers to engagement

Social and environmental responsibility is clearly an issue that SMEs believe to be important. Not only does much of the previous research indicate this, but in this most recent research 86 per cent of SMEs believe that organisations like themselves should pay significant attention to their social and environmental responsibilities. Two in three SMEs also believe this contributes to a more successful business, although a quarter disagrees. The perception of importance and a link to business success is higher among larger SMEs and those who are members of more business networks and associations. In fact, 81 per cent of organisations with 100 or more employees believe CSR activities contribute to a successful business (and only 9 per cent disagree). In addition, over nine in ten (91 per cent of SMEs) would describe their business as socially and environmentally responsible, and an even higher proportion believe their organisation has responsible business practices. Discussions with SMEs

reveal that while CSR activities are seen as part of responsible business practice, this term is most likely to conjure up thoughts of quality standards and procedures.

Key motivations are seen to be personal interest, 'just about good business practice', internal benefits of morale and motivation, giving something back (to the local community) and developing a good business image or reputation. Personal fulfilment for those involved is also a key driver and an added benefit. It should be noted that these are not only drivers for initial but also continued engagement. Philanthropy should also not be dismissed – whether because they had 'had a good year', a guilty conscience, or are keen to address issues of importance to senior management (e.g. local football team or a charity that they have a personal interest in). 'Business Community Connections' research (2002) suggests that SME involvement in community causes is driven by the philanthropic wishes of owners and senior management and is not seen as commercially important. The Small Business Service seems to agree by concluding that responsible business activity is often driven by the personal values and frame of mind of the owner and senior management (Irwin, 2002).

While the value of good publicity and improving image and reputation is recognised, in practice this seems to be seen as a result not a motivator, particularly given the fact that most SMEs do not have external shareholder influence. Similarly, greater networking opportunities are seen as an important influencer and consequence of engagement.

A significant catalyst seems to be larger businesses as customers of SMEs: 60 per cent say a large corporate customer has asked the SME to satisfy them on health and safety practices, and 43 per cent say they have had this call on environmental practices. However, only one in six (16 per cent) say this has been true for their social or community commitment.

However, a number of smaller businesses in the group discussions expressed concern about this pressure, seeing it as reducing the fun and fulfilling aspect of engagement and encouraging more bureaucracy at a cost of greater impact. There was real concern that this would put off other businesses. However, there is clearly a role for large organisations to promote and influence SMEs (as opposed to enforcing), in combination with trusted service providers and intermediaries.

In addition to leveraging third parties to involve SMEs, we know that business brokerage networks can be key in supporting engagement. The research shows that there are SME owner-managers – possibly the 'DIYers' or 'One-Offs' described earlier – who can be galvanised into action by local issues, business survival threats or requests for charitable help.

Brokerage networks (given the positive impact on social capital relative to the level of investment) could play an important role in engaging individuals from these groups and focusing their involvement with coherent initiatives.

As relationships for SMEs are different from those in large businesses (characterised by a high level of informality), this should be taken into account by intermediaries who tend to adopt a 'big business' framework in designing initiatives targeting SMEs, creating a counter-productive administrative burden. It has been shown that SMEs will attempt to avoid this burden unless the positive benefits of compliance are proven and the administrative burden reduced. Therefore, a coherent business case, drawing on the commonalities from relevant case studies, would be more effective. Encouragement is certainly seen as the preferred method through active partnerships and case studies.

Financial and tax incentives have potential and could be aligned with current policy directions, but there is concern about the difficulty of defining the activity (as reinforced through this research) and therefore enforcing an inflexible framework. There is also a feeling that incentives are often regarded with suspicion, as they can create unfair competition where an incentive is more readily available to one sector of the business community than to another. The Small Business Service (2001) concludes that tax credits are not critical as there is too much of a lag effect to be an effective incentive and the fact that more sophisticated SMEs are already likely to be maximising their tax position.

Accreditation, endorsement and awards are supported by a majority of SMEs (according to the MORI, 2000, research – 69 per cent) and gratefully received by active SMEs supportive of the marketing and relationship opportunities afforded by this. However, there is a concern that such schemes are a stronger driver for large organisations. The down-side of endorsements is seen to be additional pressure and paperwork on companies and even 'breeding bureaucracy' (The Federation of Small Businesses, in Department of Trade and Industry, 2002).

The main barriers to engagement are seen by SMEs to be cost, lack of time and resources and bureaucracy. These issues are not new, and referred to by nearly every previous publication focused on this area.

However, in-depth evaluation in this project indicates that this is often challenged by SMEs who are engaged, suggesting this is perceptual fear not reality. The group discussions also identified another major barrier – lack of awareness that this is not just 'goodwill' but an essential part of responsible business practice and a lack of understanding of the positive impact responsible business practice can have. This suggests that any tools to engage SMEs should not only be practical, easy to use and simple but also include case studies and relevant examples.

Mechanisms for further engagement

The stated objective of this study was to understand how further to engage small and medium enterprises in community and social issues. Keeping that in mind, this section will look at suggested mechanisms, messages and mediums for engagement. This is, as throughout the chapter, based on advice from third parties and from SMEs themselves – through both the qualitative and quantitative research undertaken specifically for this project.

The first key recommendation is to 'Keep It Simple' – referring not only to the terminology and language used, but also to the communication networks themselves. There is a clear feeling of bombardment (whether it be legislation or approaches from local charities) and too many organisations overlapping in advice. On issues such as community, social and environmental responsibility SMEs do not want to necessarily see yet another body emerge, and would prefer effective collaboration among network organisations and collective signposting for further advice or information. They expect to be able to network with other organisations, learn about current and best practice, the issues considered to be important and how to get started.

Involvement of sector bodies or trade associations is also key. This was regularly mentioned by SMEs throughout the group discussions, as a useful source of information. Engaged SMEs also like the idea of trade or industry associations advising companies on the key issues for their industry and how SMEs could help. This was seen as a real fit with the business and a chance to understand more about their industry and invest in long-term issues.

Sector-based CSR networks can also be valuable in promoting SME engagement. Participants in the group discussions identified a number of different mechanisms that would help them to engage further and integrate their activities into mainstream activities. It is clear that no one mechanism will engage all organisations and most request a variety from which they can pick and choose the most relevant and effective for them.

The preferred tool, mentioned spontaneously in all of the group discussions and mentioned by over three in five of SMEs in the quantitative research (partly among larger SMEs), is a checklist of issues needing business engagement. While most organisations spontaneously focus on the local area and their personal interest, there is also interest (and involvement) in sector issues (particularly manufacturing and the chemical or plastics industries) and in issues that directly threaten their business survival. This confirms the approach outlined in *Everybody's Business*, in which Grayson and Hodges (2001) propose that certain situations – either in the business itself or in the environment where it operates – can act as 'triggers' which engage an SME owner-manager with social responsibility issues. These include:

- *Sector-related circumstances* can influence which 'responsible business' issues and practices are most salient for owner-managers.
- *Business survival threats* can also influence SMEs.
- *Local networks or initiatives* such as town or regional development plans, local charity networks or business brokerage schemes can also provide incentives for SME engagement.

As SMEs focus on a checklist of issues as the most useful mechanism to aid more strategic and considered involvement, the model shown in Figure 6.2 outlines how this could be presented. Although the issues

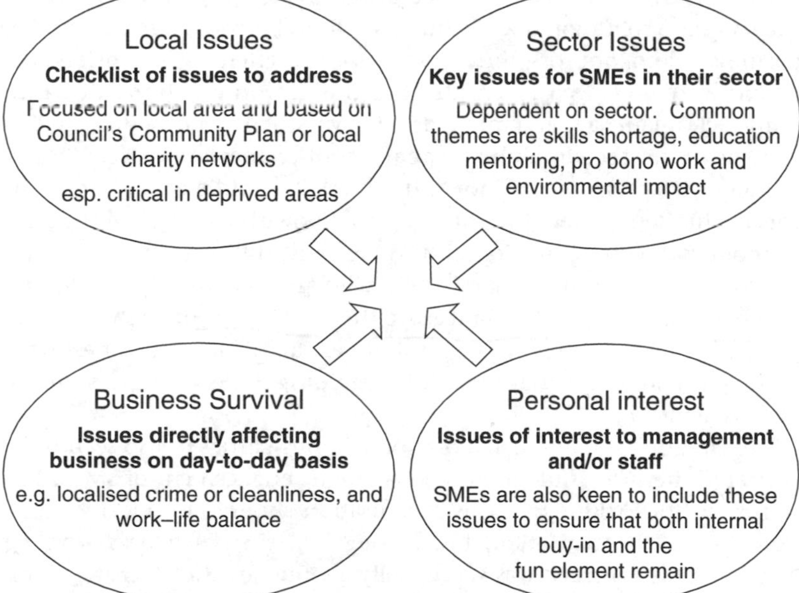

Figure 6.2 Triggers for SME engagement

themselves would need to be tailored by region and industry sector, there are clearly commonalities. This simple model allows for the fact that different triggers will engage different businesses, and ensures that a more strategic approach is adopted.

Over two in five SMEs also suggested the following could help aid further engagement:

- Advice on the business benefits (generic and actual case studies).
- Guidelines on how to get involved (under impact area headings).
- Range of case studies (in group discussions it was suggested that these would be most effective if focused on their local area and sector).
- Advice through a collaborative web-based service.

The latter could take the form of a web portal through which advice, guidelines and case studies could be accessed directly by interested SMEs as well as by third-party organisations that are promoting their engagement. However, it should be noted that a web-based resource will not access all smaller organisations. In fact, according to the Forum for Private Business only three in five SMEs have access to the Internet.

The existing CSR networks could also provide a high level of experience on the application of guidelines and tools by both large and smaller businesses and not-for-profit organisations. There is a considerable opportunity and need to ensure that this learning is translated into simple, clear language and methods. The work of AccountAbility (2002a) in revising its accountability management framework, AA1000, and producing a special module for SMEs in 2002, could play an important part in this. One other opportunity is to link with the work of the New Economics Foundation, Poptel and AccountAbility (AccountAbility, 2002b), as well as CSR Europe (2002), who are all currently developing web-based tools for SMEs to measure their social responsibility. Larger companies are also seen as useful in engaging local businesses in particular issues or initiatives, and in guiding SMEs in more strategic involvement.

The commitment and collaboration of third parties is also seen to be critical to the successful and more systematic engagement of SMEs. The consensus for SMEs is that this organisation should not, ideally, come from just one organisation, but through all their networks working together. This approach was successfully adopted by the diversity organisations (Commission for Racial Equality, Equal Opportunities Commission, NDC (New Deal for Communities – a key programme in the UK government's strategy to tackle multiple deprivation in the most deprived neighbourhoods in the country) and Equality NorthWest) by creating a greater partnership, and coordinated communication with SMEs. Through this approach they produced a central resource, checklists, guidance and practical guides.

Summary and recommendations

The vast majority of small and medium sized enterprises believe that organisations like themselves should pay significant attention to their social and environmental responsibilities. The perception of importance and a link to business success is higher among larger SMEs and those who are members of more business networks and associations. In addition, 91 per cent of SMEs would describe their business as socially and environmentally responsible, and an even higher proportion believes their organisation operates responsible business practices.

The varying nature of relationships between small and medium sized organisations and their significant stakeholders will determine the most effective mechanisms for supporting their socially responsible business practices. As relationships for smaller organisations are different from those for large businesses, this should be taken into account by intermediaries who tend to (or are seen to) adopt a 'big business' framework in designing initiatives targeting SMEs, creating a counter-productive administrative burden. Organisations seeking to engage SMEs need to be encouraged – in short, to 'Think Small First'. The values of SME owner-managers – particularly those associated with their motivation for being in business – can also provide useful clues for tailoring strategies to engage them.

SMEs' social and community activities are fragmented and informal and few have, or feel the need for, formal policies or stated intentions. Many companies are engaged with at least part of the CSR umbrella, often not knowing this is what they are doing. A key to further engagement seems to be to not only concentrate on engaging new businesses, but also to widen the engagement already active across the CSR agenda.

Overall, SMEs tend to be most focused on internal issues. Many of their responsible business practices therefore concentrate on staffing issues, increasing employee skills, and team building, as well as on morale and motivation within the organisation. Much of their social, community and environmental initiatives are therefore driven by, focused or designed to impact on, employees.

Drivers of both initial and continuing SME engagement include personal interest and fulfilment, a desire to implement 'just good business practice', improved morale and motivation, giving something back to the local community and enhancing business reputation.

Encouragement and supportive persuasion is seen as the preferred (and from the experienced, the most effective) mechanism of engagement. Promoting a sense of fun is seen as key to engaging SMEs and therefore a formalised, compulsory framework is likely to change the nature of SME activities and deter others from becoming involved.

Note

1. This publication has been adapted by Clare Southwell of Business in The Community from the 'Engaging SMEs in Community and Social Issues' Report (2002). The original report was compiled by Business in the Community, the Institute of Directors, the British Chamber of Commerce and AccountAbility. Thank you to these institutions for permission to reproduce the work here.

References

AccountAbility, *AA1000 Series: AA1000S Modules*, www.accountability.org.uk/aa1000/default.asp?pageid = 46, (2002a), accessed September 25, 2002.

AccountAbility, *Research: Virtual Exchange*, www.accountability.org.uk/research/default.asp?pageid = 27, (2002b), accessed September 25, 2002.

Business Community Connections, *Connecting SMEs with the Community: A Research Report on the Involvement of Small and Medium Sized Enterprises (SMEs) in Community Causes*, www.bcconnections.org.uk/research_report1.asp, (2002), accessed September 25, 2002.

Business in the Community, The British Chambers of Commerce, Institute of Directors and AccountAbility, *Engaging SMEs in Community & Social Issues* (London: Department of Trade and Industry, 2002).

CSR Europe, SME Key Website, www.smekey.org/, (2002), accessed September 25, 2002.

Department of Trade and Industry, *Small and Medium Sized Enterprises (SME) Statistics for the UK, 2000*, www.sbs.gov.uk/statistics, (2001), accessed September 25, 2002.

Department of Trade and Industry, *DTI Research Report – Policy Interviews 2002* (London: Department of Trade and Industry, 2002).

Forum of Private Business, *FPB Discussion Paper – Responsible Business 2002* (London: Department of Trade and Industry, 2002).

Grayson, D. and A. Hodges, *Everybody's Business: Managing Risks and Opportunities in Today's Global Society* (London: Dorling Kindersley, 2001).

Grayson, D. and D. Irwin, 'Educating Entrepeneurs', RSA lecture, 21 November (2001), London.

Howells, K., *Business and Society: Developing Corporate Social Responsibility in the UK* (London: Department of Trade and Industry, 2001).

Irwin, D., *Encouraging Responsible Business*, Small Business Service (London: Department of Trade and Industry, 2002).

Mazars Neville Russell Research, *Trends in Corporate Social Responsibility Among Mid-Corporates (£100 million to £500 million turnover)* (London: Mazars Neville Russell Research, 2001).

MORI, *SMEs' Attitudes to Social Responsibility* (London: MORI, 2000).

Small Business Service, *Regular Survey of Small Business' Opinions, First Survey – Final Report August 2001* (Birmingham: Databuild, 2001).

7 Corporate Citizenship and SMEs in Germany: A New Institutional Economics Perspective

Frank Maaß

Philanthropic involvement on the part of private individuals and, especially, also of enterprises – commonly referred to as 'corporate citizenship' – is a major contributory factor to the well-being of society in Germany. In times of decreasing budgets in the public sector, the initiators of social and environmental projects as well as those of cultural events depend increasingly on this support. From this point of view it is pleasing to observe that enterprises are discovering the advantages of corporate citizenship more and more for their business.

Let us, for instance, consider the sponsor-lists of major cultural or sporting events. The names of large enterprises are most common. It would be wrong, however, to assume that corporate citizenship is basically the domain of large enterprises, as the latest survey of the Institute for Small and Medium Sized Enterprises in Bonn (IfM Bonn) highlights. The intention of this chapter is to shed more light on the totality of responsible business practices in Germany with special emphasis on small and medium sized enterprises (SMEs). This chapter begins with an examination of research findings on corporate philanthropy in Germany. Special emphasis has been put on answering the question as to what benefits enterprises hope to reap and to what extent. To acquire a broader understanding of the pragmatic and strategic value of corporate citizenship the analysis refers to the theories of New Institutional Economics. The discussion will lead to suggestions of new ways to further the commitment of enterprises to corporate citizenship.

The data originate from two inquiries carried out by IfM Bonn in the second half of the year 2001. All activities that enterprises have undertaken voluntarily with the explicit intention to support society were considered to be philanthropic involvement. This involvement has to be kept separate from other activities primarily undertaken for business reasons – for instance, providing jobs and investing in work-related skills – even though they also have positive secondary consequences on society. Additional obligations to which enterprises by dint of law have to adhere – for example, releasing employees from work in order to participate in union activities – have not been considered.

Strategic approaches of SME corporate citizenship compared with large enterprises

To examine the manifestations of corporate citizenship and the reasons why enterprises undertake such activities, 240 enterprises from manufacturing industries and the service sector were examined. SMEs with up to 499 employees were compared with large enterprises with at least 500 employees. We consider examples of corporate citizenship to fall into categories of donation of goods, services provided free of charge, lending of corporate resources, employer and employee involvement, establishing charitable foundations and money donations.

Importance of corporate citizenship in business practices

The findings suggest that approximately four out of five enterprises (82.4 per cent) in the manufacturing industry and the service sector were involved in corporate citizenship in the years between 1997 and 2001. Among those enterprises committed to corporate citizenship, most of them had been involved on a regular basis (68.4 per cent). Others were at least sporadically active. In none of the cases was there an enterprise that had had just one involvement in corporate citizenship. This shows that corporate citizenship is already popular in Germany. Very many enterprises have even integrated social concerns in their daily business operations.

Contrary to common belief, SMEs spend more on corporate citizenship relative to their financial capabilities than large enterprises. As shown in Table 7.1, SMEs with up to 99 employees spend on average up to 0.25 per cent of their annual turnover on corporate citizenship, while this share drops drastically when enterprises of larger size are considered.

Table 7.1 also differentiates between monetary and non-monetary donations. Again, smaller enterprises are much more involved according to their financial abilities, no matter which form of donation is considered. But there are structural differences: while among larger enterprises non-monetary donations amount on average to approximately one-quarter

Table 7.1 Investments in corporate citizenship and in percentage terms of the turnover in the year 2000, according to size of enterprise

Enterprises with . . . employees	*Average expenditure on corporate citizenship (in Euros)*					
	Monetary donations		*Non-monetary donations*		*Donations altogether*	
	Total (in €1 000)	*% of turnover*	*Total (in €1 000)*	*% of turnover*	*Total (in €1 000)*	*% of turnover*
Up to 19	1.2	0.11	1.3	0.12	2.5	0.23
20 to 99	8.1	0.14	7.7	0.11	15.2	0.25
100 to 499	23.3	0.06	5.8	0.01	29.1	0.07
500 and more	206.2	0.04	64.9	0.01	271.1	0.05
Enterprises altogether (n = 188)	82.2	0.05	26.3	0.02	108.5	0.07

Table 7.2 Development of expenses for corporate citizenship between 1997 and 2001, according to size of enterprise

Enterprises with . . . employees	*Share of enterprises that . . . within five years (in %)*		
	reduced their corporate citizenship expenses	*kept their corporate citizenship expenses constant*	*increased their corporate citizenship expenses*
Up to 19	0.0	82.8	17.2
20 to 99	2.6	71.8	25.6
100 to 499	4.6	56.3	39.1
500 and more	2.5	52.5	45.0
Enterprises altogether (n = 212)	2.8	61.3	35.8

of all expenses on corporate citizenship, they amount to almost half of the expenses among smaller enterprises with up to 99 employees. The smaller the enterprise the more often other corporate resources, apart from money, play a part in philanthropic activities.

Table 7.2 gives insight into the development of corporate citizenship activities in the years 1997 till 2001. Here again a distinction can be made between enterprises of different sizes.

Corporate citizenship expenses had fallen in only a few cases. In the majority of the observations the enterprises kept at least their expenditure stable in the medium term. This indicates that many firms provide a fixed budget for social activities. The higher the number of employees the more often it could be observed that enterprises increased their budget on corporate citizenship during this period. This might on the one hand indicate that smaller enterprises are already involved to such an extent that they are pushed to their financial limits. On the other hand this finding can indicate that larger enterprises have recently discovered corporate citizenship as a worthwhile instrument of corporate management.

Ways for enterprises to support society

In order to contribute to society, enterprises can mobilise all sorts of corporate resources. As presented in Figure 7.1 and Table 7.3, most enterprises made financial donations in the time period between 1997 and 2001. The percentage of enterprises that donated goods – mostly in

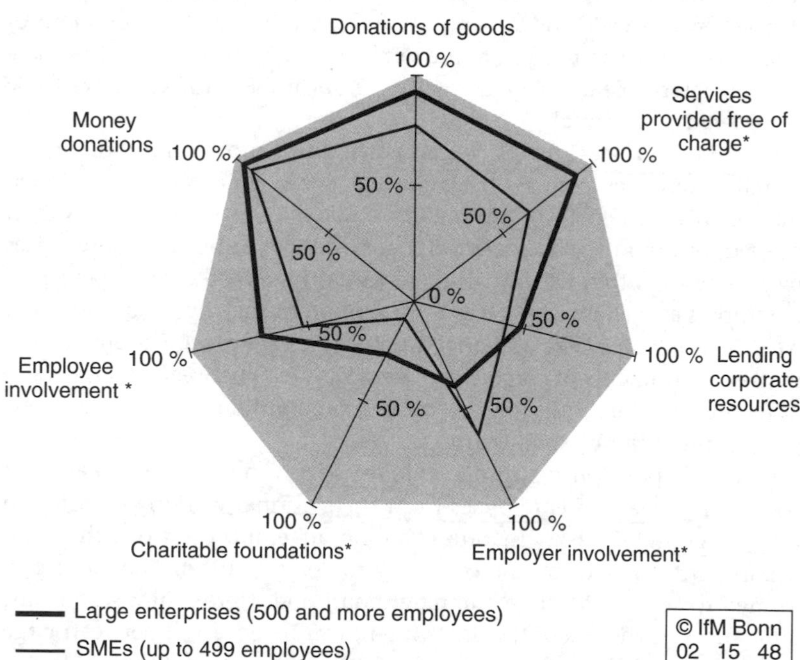

Figure 7.1 Ways of getting involved: percentage of SMEs and large firms
The data are taken from Table 7.3.
* According to a chi-square test significant differences can be observed.

Table 7.3 Ways of involvement: percentage of SMEs/large enterprises

Instruments	*Percentage of enterprises*		
	SMEs	*Large enterprises*	*All enterprises*
Money donations	94.2	94.8	94.3
Donations of goods	79.9	89.5	83.3
Services provided free of charge	70.1	88.4	76.3
Employee involvement	51.5	67.4	57.0
Employer involvement	60.4	44.2	53.5
Lending corporate resources	44.8	48.8	45.6
Charitable foundations	7.5	25.6	14.9
(n = 220)			© IfM Bonn

addition to monetary donations – was in that time-period almost as high. This included the cost-free transfer of corporate productive resources (for instance, a secondhand computer) for a good purpose. By differentiating between SMEs and large enterprises it can be seen that donations of money and goods were given to the same extent. According to a chi-square test the observable differences are not significant and thereby have to be considered as marginal.

Providing services free of charge is the third most common way by which enterprises contribute to society. Most enterprises mentioned that in this context they provide more places for apprenticeships than needed for their own business (53.9 per cent). In other cases enterprises provide services they usually compete with on the market (32.5 per cent). Enterprises also allow employees from non-profit-making organisations to participate in corporate vocational training (12.3 per cent). The application of these instruments of corporate citizenship varies between enterprises of different sizes: such services are offered predominantly by large enterprises rather than by smaller firms.

In fourth position we find employee involvement. This means the temporary release of employees from their normal working contract to fulfil honourable tasks. In one example an employee from the legal department was sent by the company to assist a citizens' action group formed to stop violence in the neighbourhood. Here again, significant differences in the use of this instrument can be observed between large enterprises and SMEs: more large enterprises are involved than SMEs.

As far as the involvement of employees is concerned, it can be seen that the ideas for such activities mostly come from the participating employees themselves. Only rarely does the initiative come from management level. Secondment programmes, where employees and sometimes even the entire staff of a department are asked to work together on charity projects, are not commonplace among enterprises in Germany. According to the findings of Janning and Bertjes (1999, p. 6), systematic releases on the basis of such programmes are much more common in other countries like the United Kingdom, the Netherlands and the United States of America.

Not only employees but also the employers themselves are personally involved in corporate citizenship. For example, in some cases employers hold an honorary function in a committee at the local Chamber of Commerce. Entrepreneurs also give lectures, for example, at schools to inform pupils about the merits of being self-employed. In comparison with large enterprises it is the employers of SMEs that personally get involved more often. In general, entrepreneurs are significantly more often involved than employed managers.

Furthermore, it could be observed that about half of the enterprises involved in corporate citizenship lend corporate resources for good and worthy purposes. In one case, for instance, an enterprise allowed children of the neighbourhood to use the firm-owned sports field. Vehicles are also lent, and corporate buildings opened for art exhibitions. Here no significant differences between enterprises of different size can be determined.

Some organisations establish their own charitable foundations. Such initiatives can rarely be observed among SMEs; this is a domain of large enterprises. This is due to the fact that mostly only large enterprises have the financial possibilities to maintain such institutions.

Fields of charity

Enterprises mostly consider social issues as the object of their philanthropic activities. Statistical evidence relating to differences in the behaviour of SMEs and large enterprises cannot be identified. Table 7.4, displaying the share of enterprises involved in different fields of charity, indicates further that cultural and educational activities come in second position among the different options that companies have to demonstrate corporate citizenship. This field is regarded with some importance primarily by larger enterprises. Supporting sport ranks as the third most popular among enterprises of all sizes. Larger enterprises also support scientific institutions. Less importance is given to environmental issues. Here again the share of large enterprises exceeds that of the SMEs.

In general, it can be observed that SMEs as well as large enterprises select fields of charity that also fit into their communication strategy.

Table 7.4 Involvement in different fields of charity, according to size of enterprise

Fields	*Share of enterprises with . . . employees (in %)*				*Enterprises altogether*
	Up to 19	*20 to 99*	*100 to 499*	*500 and more*	
Social issues	86.2	79.5	84.8	93.0	87.3*
Cultural events and education	55.2	69.2	77.3	88.4	77.3**
Sports	58.6	56.4	77.3	64.0	65.9
Scientific	17.2	25.6	37.9	64.0	43.2**
Environment	20.7	23.1	22.7	46.5	31.8**
(n = 220)					© IfM Bonn

* Requirement to calculate a chi-square test is not given.
** According to a chi-square test on the 1% level significant differences can be observed.

For instance, enterprises that often support sporting activities try to reach a wide range of their target groups in their leisure time. Firms that support either scientific or environmental issues document their target group awareness of ecological problems. It can be concluded that philanthropic activities are also determined by the specific markets in which enterprises operate. On the whole, patterns of corporate philanthropy reflect patterns of corporate interests. In addition it has to be mentioned that a majority of enterprises combine different activities of corporate citizenship.

Strategic aims

Most enterprises – and especially the large ones – consider ethical reasons as the most important driving force for their philanthropic involvement (see Figure 7.2). But whenever enterprises' commitment is based on ethical ideas they also follow business-related ideas at the same time. This leads to the conclusion that enterprises never act solely in an altruistic manner when they decide to enter the field of charity. These findings agree with results discussed by Spence and Rutherfoord (2002, p. 29) who also found that enterprises have multiple reasons for undertaking social activities.

Taking a more detailed look at the business-related aspects of corporate citizenship, it becomes evident that enterprises are fully aware of the positive links between philanthropic involvement and market performance. As Figure 7.2 shows, many enterprises aim to enhance their image and business reputation. The higher the number of employees

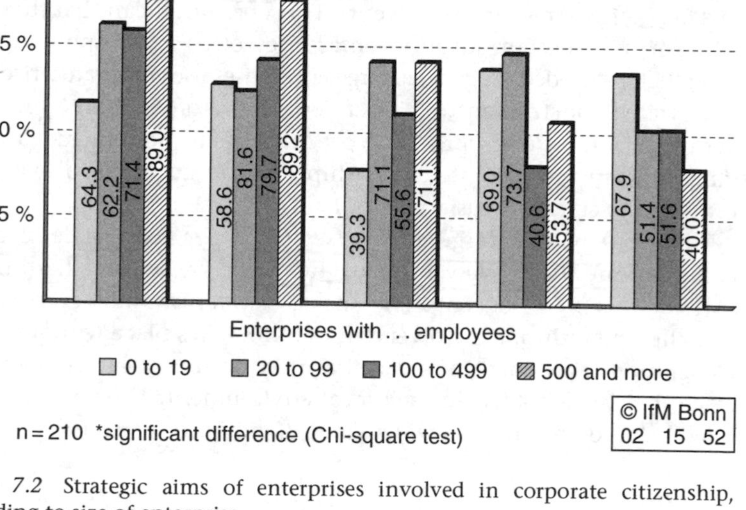

Figure 7.2 Strategic aims of enterprises involved in corporate citizenship, according to size of enterprise

the more weight enterprises give to this aim. In all of these cases corporate citizenship is regarded as an investment in their relationship to their clients and other stakeholders.

Personnel-related interests come in third position in this ranking. Larger enterprises in particular aim to improve their relationship to their own employees. If employees identify with the social involvement of their firm, this might improve their job satisfaction and encourage them to become loyal and open towards management. By signalling ethical awareness to the public, enterprises also hope to attract top job candidates. Corporate citizenship stands for an 'open culture' of the enterprise (Wagner, 1999, p. 50).

Many enterprises also aim to increase their sales. SMEs in particular often mention the intention to attract a wider public awareness as a consequence of their involvement in social activities. Many small enterprises have only limited possibilities to attract public attention. Advertisements are often unaffordable.

Last but not least, personal interests also play a crucial role in the decision process leading to an involvement in corporate citizenship. The involvement of small enterprises often depends on the personal preferences of the owners themselves.

Strategic approach

A majority of the enterprises integrate corporate citizenship in the concept of a business strategy (69.6 per cent). This does not mean that they plan all their activities in advance; enterprises often react spontaneously when help is needed. In general, large enterprises use corporate citizenship as a strategic instrument (83.3 per cent) more often than SMEs (61.4 per cent). Almost one-third (30.4 per cent) of all those included in the sample practises corporate citizenship only on an informal basis and restricted to certain occasions.

Three out of four large enterprises (76.2 per cent) at least partly communicate their involvement to the public. Little more than half of SMEs do this (52.3 per cent). This shows that in just under every second case the philanthropic involvement of SMEs takes place without public recognition. This does not mean that they do not make an attempt to reach their stakeholders in their local environment. They contact them directly but do not reach a wider circle of groups or persons.

Benefits

In general, enterprises are satisfied with their corporate citizenship involvement (94.2 per cent). Most of the enterprises perceive public acceptance of corporate citizenship to be high (84.0 per cent). What prevents enterprises from becoming involved further is uncertainty about legal matters and insufficient recognition from public administration (51.0 per cent). In many cases employees appreciate the social involvement of their firm (68.9 per cent). Only in a few cases did the employees not share this belief. Over a quarter of all employers are not aware of their employees' personal perspective (26.3 per cent). In 21.5 per cent of the observations corporate involvement encourages employees to engage themselves in the fields of charity. In 18.9 per cent of the enterprises such effects could not be observed. Nevertheless, in most cases (59.6 per cent) employers were not aware of possible encouraging effects.

Determinants of involvement in corporate citizenship

The analysis up to this point leaves no doubt that strategic considerations play a key role in the philanthropic activities of enterprises. As mentioned before, the motives for involvement differ. To examine the circumstances in which enterprises are likely to get involved in social activities, a logistic regression has to be carried out. The test results reveal the relative importance of different determinants, their influence and the extent to which they contribute to the likelihood that enterprises get involved. The data basis derives from a second survey that was carried out by the IfM Bonn for the Federation of German Industry (Bundesverband der Deutschen Industrie, BDI) and Ernst & Young (BDI, 2001). The enquiry covered 957 enterprises from manufacturing industry and industry-related services from across Germany. It focused on charitable activities that are based on a regular sponsoring contract. This restriction was considered to be appropriate, since in these cases an explicit strategic intention could be expected. Corporate citizenship was regarded as one of many instruments of communication policy. The model enables us to explain the likelihood of being committed to social activities at a high level of significance (0.001-level). The distinction of whether an enterprise is involved or not could be anticipated in 86.2 per cent of the cases.

The results of the logistic regression – presented in Table 7.5 – show that not all the independent variables clearly explain the dependent

Table 7.5 Explanatory factors for the involvement in corporate citizenship (logistic regression)

Factors	*Influence*	*Regression coefficient 'β'*	*Expected 'β'*	*Significance*
Structural factors				
• Number of employees in 2000 (logarithm)	/	–0.05	0.96	0.634
• Enterprise led by owner	/	0.22	1.24	0.482
Market performance				
• Growth rate of employees 1999 till 2000	/	0.37	1.44	0.168
• Market performance of the enterprise better than branch average (self-estimation)	/	0.48	1.61	0.077
Industry (reference category: industry related services)				
• Producer goods industry	/	–0.52	0.59	0.252
• Investment goods industry	/	–0.10	0.90	0.848
• Consumer goods industry	/	0.32	1.38	0.455
• Building industry	+	1.04	2.83	0.038*
Target markets				
• Industry	–	–0.54	0.58	0.049*
• Craft	/	–0.10	0.91	0.757

Table 7.5 (Continued)

Factors	*Influence*	*Regression coefficient 'β'*	*Expected 'β'*	*Significance*
• Trade	/	–0.26	0.77	0.361
• Services	/	0.03	1.03	0.931
• Public sector	/	–0.09	0.91	0.765
• Ultimate consumers	+	0.91	2.49	0.014*
Instruments of communication policy				
• Direct consultations with clients	/	0.27	1.31	0.479
• Advertising via media	/	–0.14	0.87	0.680
• Direct advertising (mailings etc.)	/	0.48	1.62	0.074
• Informal contacts to clients	+	0.70	2.01	0.013*
• Presentation at fairs	–	–0.64	0.53	0.032*
• Exhibitions, organised by the enterprise	+	0.63	1.88	0.035*
• Public relations	++	1.14	3.14	0.000***
• Presentation on public occasions	++	1.69	5.41	0.000***
Other management instruments				
• Guarantee policy	–	–0.63	0.53	0.028*
• Employee participation as an instrument of personnel policy	/	–0.04	0.96	0.874
• Environmentally friendly methods of production	/	0.02	1.02	0.935
• Cooperation with other firms	++	0.88	2.41	0.001**
Constant factor	--	–4.21	---	0.000***

© IfM Bonn

Number of observations = 731.
Log-likelihood = 671.963.
Cox & Snell-R^2 = 0.254.
Significant on the 0.05 level (*), the 0.01 level (**) respectively on the 0.001 level.
+(++) variable has a positive (highly positive) influence.
–(--) variable has a negative (highly negative) influence.
/ variable has no significant influence.

variable: the analysis indicates that neither the size of an enterprise nor the way it is managed – whether it be by the owner or management – are determinants for the willingness or the ability of a firm to enter into corporate citizenship activities.

In addition, the data provide no evidence to support the assumption that there is a connection between the current economic performance of an enterprise and the likelihood of getting involved in corporate citizenship. It is suggested that not only expanding firms are involved in corporate citizenship, but also those with a stagnating or even decreasing number of employees. This finding is also reflected in the way the firms view themselves. Enterprises that regard themselves as relatively successful compared with their competitors do not necessarily show a greater involvement in corporate citizenship than firms that are not performing so well. This indicates that the motivation to support society to a great extent does not depend on the short-term market performance of a firm. A pro-cyclical behaviour cannot be observed.

The model further suggests that the field of activity of an enterprise will have an influence on the enterprise's participation in corporate citizenship. Socially orientated business practices can be observed significantly more often among enterprises in the construction sector than among enterprises in other sectors in the manufacturing industry. This result supports the conclusion that sector-specific customer relations influence the profitability of philanthropic activities. As the model shows, enterprises that focus on the demands of their private consumers are much more likely to be active in the fields of corporate citizenship than others are. This specifies the positive premise of the regression coefficient in Table 7.4. In addition, it can be stated that industrial suppliers tend to be less involved in social issues.

To come to a broader understanding of the logic behind philanthropic activities, the instrument mix of communication policy of the enterprises needs to be analysed more closely. Enterprises that invest in public relations in general will be more committed to philanthropic activities. Socially related business practice is often combined with elements of information policy. It seems more than rational that enterprises that also support society have an interest in communicating their involvement to the public. But there is more to it than that: both instruments are implemented in order to influence public opinion, to enhance the image of the enterprise and, at the same time, improve its relations to certain social groups. This explains the implementation of both instruments and their complementary character. For the same reasons, philanthropic activities are often pooled together with sales promotion and public presentations.

All these instruments which are mainly used in combination with corporate citizenship have one thing in common: they are addressed to a large and anonymous public. It is interesting that enterprises that strive to take up direct contact with potential clients at fairs are not so inclined to participate in corporate citizenship. Enterprises that operate in markets where they usually have close ties or can contact potential clients relatively easily are less committed to corporate citizenship for strategic reasons. These enterprises usually know their market partners and do not depend on advertising platforms addressed to a vast mass of potential clients. That also explains why industrial suppliers are less inclined to undertake philanthropic activities. This does not mean that industrial suppliers are not interested in improving their image and are not concerned about social issues, but that they do not appear to be dependent on this instrument of communication policy as much as others.

The results of the logistic regression shed light on further links between responsible business practice and the usage of other management instruments. But the intention of this chapter was not to analyse in depth all of the findings of the study (for subsequent discussions, see Maaß and Clemens, 2002, p. 37). To analyse the discourse on the strategic role of philanthropic involvement only one aspect should be emphasised: as the regression indicates, enterprises which put an emphasis on guarantees to their clients (e.g. warranty certificates, after-sale services) as an instrument of their business policy will in general be less committed to corporate citizenship than those not focusing on this firm policy.

It cannot be assumed that both policies are in stark contrast to each other. Rather, the negative link between them is an indication that these instruments are being used for different purposes. Guarantee policy is surely designed to reduce business risks. Both approaches serve the same business interests: they are implemented to improve the relationship between the enterprise and its customers. As stressed above, the fostering of relationships between market partners can also be achieved by corporate citizenship. Therefore it is evident that policies relating to reputation, guarantee and information – schematically presented in Figure 7.3 – are closely related and connected with each other.

To analyse further the role of these instruments and the conditions in which enterprises avail themselves of one or the other, we have to study more closely the nature of the relationships between enterprises and their market partners.

Corporate citizenship from the perspective of New Institutional Economics

In order to investigate the role of reputation in business relations, the ways in which enterprises organise their relationships to both external

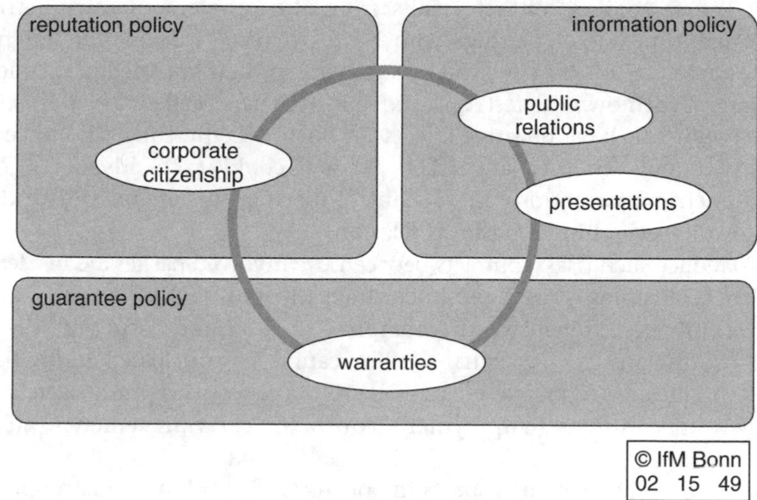

Figure 7.3 Policies of relationship management (schematic figure)

(e.g. clients, suppliers) and internal stakeholders (employees) must be regarded separately. One has to look at the business culture and the steps that need to be taken to build up and maintain such relationships. In order to fulfil this task, further discussion on the theories of New Institutional Economics (NIE) is needed.

Fundamental for these theoretical approaches is the methodological perspective of individualism (Richter and Furubotn, 1999, p. 3). Enterprises are regarded as organisations in which individuals with different preferences and interests cooperate. This point of view opens a new perspective also on interactions between enterprises, their clients and other stakeholders. Again these relations are characterised by different interests (Wolff, 1999, p. 134). It can be assumed that all players within these business relations are normally willing to make arrangements in order to satisfy their expectations. In this process the reciprocal exchange of information plays a crucial role. New Institutional Economics acknowledges that in reality each party involved in many cases lacks relevant information about its partners. For instance, how could a client know whether a potential supplier would be cooperative in the event of problems with the product that may occur after the purchase? How can an employer be sure that employees will act in the expected way when there is no direct control?

A key factor for conflict results from the problem of asymmetric information. Market partners who have exclusive information might take advantage of this situation by suppressing their knowledge in order to pursue their own interests more effectively. The so-called opportunistic behaviour can have negative effects on business efficiency. The uncertainty about whether a market partner could take advantage of asymmetric information can – if control mechanisms are missing or do not work – even hinder business relations.

To reduce such risks, contracts between the involved parties are needed. But in reality – as is discussed in contract theory – such agreements are never fully comprehensive and complete (Richter and Furubotn, 1999, p. 247). In many cases potential conflicts cannot be anticipated during the time business relations are established. As a consequence, only sketchily drawn-up contracts (employment contracts, sales agreements, etc.) are made.

It is normal that many aspects in contracts of this kind remain open: the partners in such relationships depend on trust. Mutual acceptance and confidence in each other's reliability must be considered to be of paramount importance in business relations. An atmosphere of trust provides safety for all partners so that possible conflicts can be settled by mutual agreement. Wagner regards mutual trust as an economic resource (1999, p. 56).

To be considered trustworthy is a substantial part of corporate reputation. Spremann stresses that reputation can reduce risk-related transaction costs (1989, p. 742). Such a reputation can also be established by a good communications policy, e.g. image campaigns (public relations). It can be built up by charitable activities, thus documenting willingness to act in accordance with basic moral rules. This again requires an open attitude of the firms for the concerns of market partners and other social groups. Habisch and Schmidpeter argue that trust and reciprocally accepted norms can only be reached by an ongoing communication process with the environment (2001, p. 14). Consequently, by showing a willingness to take the interests of others into account when decisions are made,  a trustworthy atmosphere can be created. The two authors quoted above highlight that moral behaviour is a factor that stabilises reciprocal behavioural expectations (ibid., p. 17).

On the basis of these considerations the negative link between guarantee- and reputation-policy on the one hand and the positive link between information- and reputation-policy on the other – as concluded from the empirical findings – seems plausible. The less enterprises are able to provide guarantees and thereby reduce business risks, e.g. because they mainly supply non-standardised products or services, the more they are interested in closing this gap by signalling their reliability through a philanthropic involvement.

The demonstration of moral attitudes can help to create an atmosphere of trust in inter-enterprise relations: it may also reduce the risks of opportunistic behaviour on the part of individuals working within a firm.

Conclusions and political implications

Corporate citizenship is first of all an economic activity, but it has social dimensions as well (Himmelstein, 1997, p. 3). Corporate citizenship in most cases must not be regarded as an optional attachment to business core activities, but as a part of the organisational philosophy and business approach. In order to build up mutual trust, such an attitude can be signalled by corporate citizenship activities. An atmosphere of trust is the basis of stable relations between enterprises and stakeholders. Most enterprises in Germany – SMEs nearly as often as large ones – realise the benefits deriving from social involvement. Almost all of the enterprises consider their activities as being successful, and corporate citizenship activities find an overall positive awareness in the German public.

The variety of philanthropic activities indicates that the firms are not lacking in creative ideas to support others. Promoting good practices can encourage enterprises to intensify their corporate citizenship involvement even more. Additional bureaucracy, for instance an obligation to report such activities, would be a burden on the enterprises. Such impositions can be counterproductive and prevent enterprises from a greater involvement in corporate citizenship.

The main barrier to corporate citizenship is to be found in the uncertainties in legislative matters. Many ideas were never put into practice because of a lack of information about legal issues. Cost-free counselling services would be much appreciated. Existing advisory boards at an administrative level should be organised more efficiently. Many enterprises complain that contactors are difficult to find or that such specialists in many cases are not well informed. Functioning networks are needed, so that enterprises can be referred to that person or institution that is qualified to provide advice. Engaging more enterprises requires guidelines that help start and develop their own models of charity. Providing checklists, which can be downloaded from the Internet, is regarded as an effective method to reduce existing barriers and to open doors for all those enterprises that are willing to support society.

References

BDI (Bundesverband der Deutschen Industrie e.V.) and Ernst & Young, Deutsche Allgemeine Treuhand AG Wirtschafts-Prüfungsgesellschaft, *Das industrielle Familienunternehmen – Kontinuität im Wandel*, BDI-Drucksache no. 331 (Berlin, 2001).

Habisch, A. and R. Schmidpeter, 'Social Capital, Corporate Citizenship and Constitutional Dialogues – Theoretical Considerations for Organisational Strategy', in A. Habisch, H.-P. Meister and R. Schmidpeter (eds), *Corporate Citizenship as Investing in Social Capital* (Berlin: Logos-Verlag, 2001).

Himmelstein, J., *Looking Good and Doing Good. Corporate Philanthropy and Corporate Power* (Indianapolis: Indiana University Press, 1997).

Janning, H. and H. Bertjes, *Ehrenamt und Wirtschaft. Internationale Beispiele bürgerschaftlichen Engagements der Wirtschaft*, Beiträge zum Ehrenamt no. 2 (Stuttgart: Robert Bosch Stiftung, 1999).

Maaß, F. and R. Clemens, *Corporate Citizenship: Das Unternehmen als 'guter Bürger'*, Schriften zur Mittelstandsforschung no. 94 NF, Bonn (2002).

Richter, R. and E.G. Furubotn, *Neue Institutionenökonomik: Eine Einführung und kritische Würdigung* (Tübingen: Mohr Siebeck, 1999).

Spence, L.J. and R. Rutherfoord, 'Soziale Verantwortung, Gewinnmaximierung und der KMU-Unternehmer/Geschäftsführer', *Zeitschrift für Klein- und Mittelunternehmen*, Swiss Research Institute of Small Business and Entrepreneurship, 50(1), (2002) 17–34.

Spremann, K., 'Stakeholder-Ansatz versus Agency-Theorie', *Zeitschrift für Betriebswirtschaft*, 7, (1989) 742–5.

Wagner, A., 'Unternehmensethik in Banken', *Bankenwissenschaftliche Schriftenreihe*, 89, Vienna (1999).

Wolff, B., 'Zum methodischen Status von Verhaltensannahmen in der Neuen Institutionenökonomik', in T. Edeling, W. Jann and D. Wagner (eds), *Institutionenökonomie und Neuer Institutionalismus. Überlegungen zur Organisationstheorie*, Interdisziplinäre Organisations- und Verwaltungsforschung 2, Opladen (1999).

8

Strategies and Instruments for Organising CSR by Small and Large Businesses in the Netherlands

Johan Graafland, Bert van de Ven and Nelleke Stoffele

The focus in this chapter[1] is on the way in which businesses respond to social responsibility and how they deal with the challenges posed. A comparison is made between large and small firms in the Netherlands.

Business ethics has become a well-recognised aspect of management. Due to the increasing interest of society in responsible behaviour of firms, many firms are nowadays concerned about values like integrity and develop ethical codes to foster responsible behaviour of their employees. They feel that they must meet the 'triple P' bottom line expressing the expectations of stakeholders with respect to the firm's contribution to profit, planet and people in order to have a licence to operate.

As a result, it becomes more important for firms to integrate ethics in the organisational structure. For this purpose, a firm can use several strategies and instruments. In this chapter we research the use of these strategies and instruments by large and small enterprises in two provinces in the Netherlands. In particular, we are interested in whether there are systematic differences between large and small firms with respect to the instruments that they use to foster ethical behaviour of the firm and its employees.

There are several reasons why we expect such systematic differences. First, large firms are more visible to the public and the media. This makes investments in responsible production and selling patterns relatively more important for large firms. The same effect we expect from scale: as large firms have a larger scale, the costs involved with the development of ethical instruments like a code of conduct are relatively small. Third, because of their larger scale, large firms have more need for instruments that facilitate the communication of values and norms within the firm and to their customers. Whereas small enterprises often have personal contacts with their customers and employees, large firms relatively operate more in large and anonymous markets with many customers and work with a large pool of employees. Therefore, we would hypothesise that a large firm will make relatively more use of formal and public instruments to communicate its responsibility and to build up a consistent business culture, whereas small firms use more informal means. A fourth reason why we expect that large firms will make more use of instruments to organise corporate social responsibility (CSR) is that competition might be stronger for small enterprises than for large firms. If the competitiveness is high, any price differential caused by additional costs from social and ecological efforts is very high in terms of declining market share (Graafland, 2002a).

The content of this chapter is as follows. First, we give an overview of strategies and instruments that firms can use to stimulate ethical behaviour by its managers and employees. Then we describe the sample of our research. Following this we offer an extensive description of the outcomes. We then test our hypothesis that the scale of the firm has a significant impact on the use of different instruments. Finally, we summarise the main findings.

Organisation of ethics: strategies and instruments

To operate in a responsible way requires that managers and employees act in accordance with certain values and norms. Often, a firm has its own culture with unwritten rules that are communicated in an informal way. However, if firms grow larger, it becomes more difficult to apply informal channels to communicate the main business values and to ensure that employees act in a responsible way. Therefore, a firm needs instruments that can improve the communication of values and norms within the firm and between the firm and external stakeholders. For that purpose, the firm can follow different strategies and use various instruments.

Three strategies of organising ethics

There are several ways of defining and organising ethical behaviour. Building on the work of Sharp Paine (1994), Hummels and Karssing (2000) distinguish three types of strategies. In the first strategy – the compliance strategy – the firm develops concrete standards of behaviour, which are communicated to all members of the organisation. The focus is on required behaviour (Trevino and Nelson, 1999). Supervision of the behaviour of the managers and employees or other business partners guarantees the ethical quality of the organisation partners. Those who are found shirking are punished. This strategy requires the following steps:

- communication of standards and procedures that hold for the members of the organisation. Often these standards concern rules that are minimally required;
- supervision of the behaviour of the organisation members;
- procedures to report unethical behaviour;
- punishment of organisation members that do not follow the standards.

An example of the compliance strategy is the code of conduct and audit procedures used by C&A (see Graafland, 2002b). C&A is a large Western textile retail company. The C&A code for the supply of merchandise mainly contains concrete rules that can be checked, and clearly outline what must be done or not done. The code is communicated to all suppliers and audited by Servers Organisation for Compliance Audit Management (SOCAM). Infringements are reported by SOCAM to C&A Buying and sanctioned by suspending business (Graafland, 2002c).

The second strategy – the integrity strategy – does not rely on compliance with strict rules, but rather on the personal responsibility and integrity of the individual employees on the basis of internalised values. Integrity means that managers and employees are prepared to fulfil their tasks in a professional, accurate and responsible way, taking into account all relevant interests. In order to apply this strategy in a successful way, the firm must define clear core values and train managers and employees to apply these core values in concrete situations. In order to apply this strategy successfully, the firm must:

- define clear core values;
- train managers and employees to apply these core values in concrete situations;
- let managers have their own responsibility for which they are accountable.

For example, Levi-Strauss uses an 'aspiration statement' in which it describes its main values. This statement says, for example, that Levi-Strauss wants its people to feel respected, treated fairly, listened to and involved. These are very general values, which leave open a lot of discretion in concrete decisions.

The third strategy – the dialogue strategy – pays attention to the expectations of the stakeholders of the firm. This strategy focuses on 

responsiveness to the ideas, interests and values of others. The organisation constantly tries to learn from new situations and from what external parties communicate. This strategy requires:

- ongoing communication about moral issues with external stakeholders;
- search for information about other cultures and conventions;
- being accountable for the business actions to external stakeholders.

An example is the Shell Report Profits and Principles of 1998. This Shell Report contained a separate Tell Shell card, which the readers of the report could send back to Shell to comment on the Report. In this way, Shell informs itself about the perceptions of its external stakeholders and can adapt its policies accordingly.

In reality, the three strategies are complementary. For example, in order to fight child labour effectively, one needs an appropriate mixture of the three strategies that takes all interests, values and insights into account. If one wants to combat child labour, one should adopt an effective audit system that prevents the worst forms of child labour by suppliers. However, from a broader perspective one should be aware that a strict compliance strategy can bring children into a less favourable situation. Respecting the underlying basic values therefore sometimes requires a flexible approach by, for example, offering working children alternatives from which they really benefit, including education in combination with appropriate working times and working conditions. Finally, in order to know the needs of the children and their families, information from representative organisations like local NGOs can be helpful.

Instruments

In our research we distinguish several instruments that facilitate responsible behaviour to external and/or internal stakeholders. We define responsible behaviour as all actions directed at safeguarding the legitimate interests of the stakeholders of the firm. What constitutes a legitimate interest should be determined by a moral analysis of the interests at stake and in cases of serious disagreement by a dialogue process (Van de Ven, 1999).

First, in order to communicate the ethical standards, many firms have developed codes of conduct. A code of conduct is a document that sets out the basic responsibilities of the organisation towards its stakeholders (Sociaal Economische Raad, 2001). Research indicates that employees from firms with a code of conduct feel more encouraged and supported for ethical behaviour than employees without a code (Adams *et al.*, 2001).[2] A code of conduct can contain three types of statements: the mission statement that describes the purpose of the firm; value statements that describe the main values of the firm; and rules of conduct that describe the type of behaviour that the organisation expects from its workers or suppliers. Sometimes, a firm uses different documents for these different types of statements. When developing a code, an organisation is confronted with a series of choices (Kaptein and Wempe, 1998). For example, a code of conduct can either prescribe concrete norms or, instead, the general values of the firm. In case of a compliance strategy, the code will mainly contain rules that can be checked and clearly outline what must be done or not done. Particularly when the stakeholders have substantial interests at stake, a clear and finely outlined policy must be defined. The disadvantage of rules is that not all actions can be incorporated in them. Therefore, a code must also make explicit considerations behind the rules that enable organisation members to apply an integrity strategy in line with the basic values of the firm. Another choice concerns the stakeholders for whom the code applies. Some firms use an internal code for employees only, whereas others prefer an external code, for example for suppliers or the general public.

In order to ensure that the code of conduct is much more than simply a paper commitment, firms sometimes set up procedures to audit compliance with the code and to promote the awareness of the code. Auditing is the process in which an organisation measures, evaluates, reports and adapts its social impact and ethical behaviour in light of the values and expectations of stakeholders. For small and medium firms it is often difficult to self-organise this process. A more practical approach is to make use of existing certifications, like ISO 9001 and ISO 14001.[3] Firms can voluntarily choose to subject themselves to the judgment of independent organisations that are allowed to certify the social or environmental quality of the production processes of the firm. Whereas ISO 9001 is mostly concerned with safety issues, ISO 14001 relates to environmental aspects. The advantage of the ISO 14001 norm is the practical focus. It is a recognised global standard, open to all organisations. No initial review is necessary (McIntosh *et al.*, 1998). In order to keep the ISO certificate, each year the firm has to develop an annual ecological scheme that describes the goals and actions for improving the environmental situation. This environmental year plan specifies the items that the firm wants to improve. Besides the concrete actions to realise these targets, the year plan reports the costs per operation, the division that is responsible for the operation and the date at which the operation will be realised. Since

ISO 14001 requires improving the safety and ecological standards each year, it stimulates continuous innovation.[4] Another certificate that we include in our research is the so-called NEVI code of conduct. This certificate guarantees the position of suppliers and protects them against unethical behaviour of customers.

An instrument related to auditing is the publication of an annual social report. An outstanding example is the report of Shell. In this report Shell gives many statistics on the environment and social issues like emission of CO² and other gases, safety, operating procedures to ensure equal opportunities, gender diversity, grievance procedures, social investments and reported cases of bribery (see www.shell.com/annualreport). Independent accountancy bureaus (Price Waterhouse Coopers and KPMG) verify some of these statistics. Some firms also include social aspects in the annual financial report. For example, in their annual report Heijmans report the sickness absence rate, the number of employees that became disabled and the number of injuries specified to different types. The report also includes an overview of the volume of construction waste. Finally, it reports the remuneration of members of the board.

Whereas codes of conduct, ISO-certifications and social reports improve the accountability of the firm to external stakeholders, other instruments are particularly useful for organising the responsibility to internal stakeholders, like employees. First, an internal social handbook may clarify the position of employees by defining many rules with respect to the labour conditions of employees. Another possibility is to appoint a trusted and confidential person for employees, to whom they can communicate abuses on the shop floor when, for example, their direct boss is involved. The confidential person can provide first help to the victim, advise about the possibilities for further action, guide the process and play an intermediary role between the victim and the offender. In this way, legal procedures can sometimes be prevented and structural action undertaken to improve the situation (Kaptein and Buiter, 2001). The ethics committee, the human resource manager or a member of the workers' council can all have a similar function. The presence of an ethics committee is a clear signal to the organisation's members. In very small firms most of these instruments demand too many resources. In that case, one can stimulate the internal communication of ethical issues if the director or a member of the board explicitly takes responsibility for this. A final instrument to improve the ethical awareness in the firm is to give training to employees. This instrument is especially relevant if the firm follows an integrity strategy in which the core values are communicated. In order to be effective, one should train the employees in how to apply these core values in concrete situations.

The various instruments serve different functions. For example, codes of conduct and social handbooks explain the values and norms and thereby clarify the policy of the firm. They show what the firm expects from its management and employees. The reflection on values and norms will also help to reduce inconsistencies in firm policy. Second, a code of conduct and, in particular, ethical training empowers the moral consciousness of the employees. Third, certifications offer management tools to identify shortcomings and to improve ethical standards. Internal procedures like a confidential person and an ethics committee may stimulate managers and employees to consider the ethical values and norms. Fourth, a public code of conduct and the publication of a social report improve the dialogue with external stakeholders by communicating what they can expect from the firm. Finally, a code of conduct, certifications and the publication of a social report may also improve the external reputation of the firm if the firm is able to prove that its acts are in accordance with its code of conduct.

Sample

The goal of the research is to analyse the organisation of ethics by large and small enterprises in two Dutch provinces, North Brabant and Zeeland.[5] A standard classification of a small firm applied by the organisation for small and medium sized business in the Netherlands is a firm with less than 100 employees. Accordingly, large firms are defined as firms with 100 or more employees.[6] In order to increase the comparability between different firms, the research focuses only on four sectors: construction,  metal manufacturing, financial services and wholesale traders (Table 8.1). The focus on four sectors allows the comparison of results for different firms within one sector. Moreover, the selection facilitates detecting sector-specific characteristics.

In order to obtain the addresses of firms, the Chamber of Commerce was asked to make five random address lists. Four lists consist of 300 addresses of firms in the four sectors with fewer than one hundred employees. The fifth lists contained 318 addresses of all firms with more than one hundred employees in the four sectors.

The sample of firms that sent in a completed questionnaire consists  of 111 firms. Table 8.2 gives an overview of the response per sector.

As can be seen, the response rate was relatively low (about 15 per cent for large firms and 5 per cent for small firms). In addition, we received

Table 8.1 Sectors

Sector	*Specification*
Metal manufacturing	All firms that deal with the production of machines and appliances like office machines and computers, electronic machines appliances and requirements, audio, video, telecommunication machines and requirements, medical machines and instruments, cars and transport instruments.
Construction	All firms that deal with the building industry.
Financial services	Financial institutions, mortgage banks, construction funds and accountants.
Wholesale traders	All wholesale traders in textile products, clothing, shoes, domestic appliances, glass, Chinese pottery, wallpaper and cleansers, perfumes, cosmetics, pharmaceuticals and non-food consumer products.

Table 8.2 Number of completed questionnaires

	Large	*Small*	*Total*
Metal manufacturing	14	17	31
Construction	14	10	24
Financial services	10	17	27
Wholesalers	10	19	29
Total	48	63	111

13 incomplete responses that were not appropriate for our research. Reasons for the low response were:

- some firms ceased to exist
- addresses given by the Chamber of Commerce were not correct
- single-person firms (as the strategies and instruments are only useful for organisations with more than one person)

A phone-call three weeks after the final date of sending in the questionnaire to 40 firms that did not respond showed that most firms did not return the questionnaires either because of the discussed subject, the high work pressure or the length of the questionnaire. Indeed, besides 11 questions about the organisation of ethics and 8 questions about characteristics of the firm (see below), the questionnaire contained 75 other questions related to the vision of firms on CSR and on all kinds of practical aspects (see Graafland *et al.*, 2002).

The relatively low response rate implies that the outcomes probably do not fully represent the complete sample of 1,518 firms. Indeed, it is likely that firms that are relatively active in using instruments to foster corporate social responsibility will have been more inclined to send in the questionnaire. However, comparison with the results of other research (see Table 8.3) indicates that there is no reason to believe that this bias is very large. Nor do our results suggest that because of the lower response rate the (positive) bias would be much stronger for small than for large firms (see Table 8.3). Another question is whether the answers of the respondents reflect social response bias or the real situation. As the questionnaire was anonymous, firms had no reason to present a more favourable picture compared with the real situation. Indeed, as we will see below, many firms reported a relatively low score with respect to several instruments, indicating that the questionnaire was filled-in in an honest way.

Table 8.3 presents the average size of the firms in various sectors, both at the local level and at the national level. The first column shows that the construction and metal manufacturing firms are on average much larger if measured at the local level. However, since a relatively small share of the construction firms in the panel are a subsidiary firm of a larger firm, the size of the total firm including sister firms is relatively small for the construction sector. In contrast, the average size for metal manufacturing firms and financial services at the overall level is relatively large, as many local firms are part of a very large national firm. This is especially relevant for financial services with less than 100 employees at the local level. As 41 per cent of these firms are part of a large firm, the size of the total firm to which these small enterprises belong is much larger. Since we expect that both the size of the local firm and the size of the total firm impacts the use of instruments, we will include both variables in the econometric estimates in the following analysis.

Results

Strategies

One question in the questionnaire specifically asks which type of strategy is used by the firm to organise corporate social responsibility. The question was formulated as follows: For the organisation of corporate social responsibility in the firm we make use of: (1) fixed standards with controlling and rewarding systems, (2) stimulate the awareness of clear standards without controlling or sanctioning mechanisms, (3) a dialogue

Table 8.3 Average number of employees per firm (at the local level)

	Total (at local level)	*Large (>100 employees at local level)*			*Small (<100 employees at local level)*		
		At local level	*Of which part of larger firm*	*Including sister firms*	*At local level*	*Share of firms that are part of larger firm*	*Including sister firms*
Construction	675	1132	36%	5078	36	20%	1083
Metal manufacturing	367	787	86%	54316	21	12%	77
Financial services	83	169	50%	35614	32	41%	12312
Retail	148	396	70%	3405	17	21%	720

with stakeholders from which we determine new aspects of corporate social responsibility that we want to realise, (4) no strategy. The first option reflects the compliance strategy, the second option is used to represent the integrity strategy, the third option the dialogue strategy, whereas the last option is assumed to reflect firms that have not deliberately thought about how to integrate their ethical standards in the firm.

Table 8.4 gives an overview of the answers. The table shows that a relatively large proportion of small firms prefer a dialogue strategy with stakeholders, in particular in the construction sector. This result matches the findings of Spence *et al.* (2000). Their research focuses on the approaches of small businesses to the environment in the UK and the Netherlands. The small businesses in the Netherlands that were included in the research are all from the region of North Brabant, which makes their findings especially relevant for us. The researchers conclude that small businesses in the Netherlands make use of 'communicative processes of bargained consultation, dialogue and exchange of information, through which consensual agreements about co-operation on social problems among a plurality of partners are pursued' (Spence *et al.*, 2000, p. 958).

Larger firms consider this dialogue strategy useful as well, but tend to favour the integrity strategy, in particular in financial services and the wholesale sector. The compliance strategy is least popular. Maybe this is due to the fact that the control and rewarding of ethical behaviour requires a lot of resources. Another reason might be that the Dutch consensus culture renders a strict compliance strategy ineffective. Finally, it is noted that among smaller firms a substantial proportion of firms consider none of the three strategies as relevant. This might indicate that these firms feel that corporate social responsibility is not sufficiently relevant to require a systematic strategic approach.

Instruments

The use of different instruments was researched by ten questions. The first question asked for the use of a written mission statement or plan of policy. We find a substantial difference between large and small firms. In particular, 90 per cent of the large firms have a mission statement, against 49 per cent of the small firms. A closer look shows that the large metal manufacturing and financial firms all have a mission statement, whereas 80 per cent of the large construction firms and wholesalers do so.

More interesting for our research are the other nine questions that relate to instruments that are specifically designed to stimulate ethical behaviour. In order to investigate the current situation both from a static and a dynamic point of view, we used a similar structure of questions to

Table 8.4 Strategies of organising CSR (as a %)

Type of strategy	*Metal manufacturing*	*Construction*	*Financial services*	*Wholesale*	*Total*	*Large*	*Small*
Compliance	21	13	4	10	12	20	7
Integrity	17	17	35	41	28	40	19
Dialogue	28	44	42	21	33	27	37
Non-applicable	35	26	19	28	27	13	37
	100	100	100	100	100	100	100

Table 8.5 Instruments for organising CSR[a]

	Realised		*Planned*		*Known and useful*		*Known and not useful*		*Unknown*	
	Large	*Small*	*Large*	*Small*	*Large*	*Small*	*Large*	*Small*	*Large*	*Small*
Code of conduct	51	29	2		14	4	9	25	23	42
ISO 9001/14001 certification	76	32		6	5	4	10	43	10	15
NEVI code	6	2	2	1	3	0	5	18	27	33
Publication of annual social report	62	20	9	2	4	5	13	36	11	38
Social handbook	87	40	2	11	9	7	2	19		23
Confidential person	84	40	2	2	7	7	5	32	2	19
Ethics committee	17	7		4	7	2	29	46	48	42
Member of board is answerable for ethical issues	67	59		2	9	12	9	9	14	19
Ethical training	14	7			12	7	23	31	51	55

[a] As a percentage of the respondents.

that of Ulrich *et al.* (1998). In particular, we did not only ask for the present use of the instruments, but also whether the firm was aware of the instrument and planned to use it in the future. The results are reported in Table 8.5.

Table 8.5 shows that, on average, large firms make more use of all instruments. The most popular instruments are a social handbook and confidential person. Also ISO certifications are very common among large firms, whereas a majority use a code of conduct, publish social indicators and have a member of the board who is answerable for ethical issues. From a dynamic perspective, it can be concluded that in the future the incidence of a code of conduct and social reporting will increase. Nine per cent of the large firms have plans to introduce a social report, whereas 14 per cent of the large firms knows about codes of conduct and considers them to be a useful instrument.

Least popular are the ethics committee and ethical training options. An explanation might be that most firms already use a confidential person and therefore consider these additional instruments as over-abundant. Another explanation is that a substantial part of the large firms do not know these instruments. The same holds for the relatively new NEVI code of conduct for suppliers.

As already mentioned, Table 8.5 confirms our hypothesis that small firms are less inclined to use formal instruments to foster ethical behaviour within the organisation than are large firms. As noted in the introduction, there are several reasons that explain such systematic differences. First, large firms are more visible to the public and the media. This makes investments in external communication patterns like a code of conduct, ISO certification and social reporting relatively more important for large firms. Second, as large firms have a larger scale, the costs involved with the development of ethical instruments are relatively small. Third, because of their larger scale, large firms have a greater need for instruments that facilitate the communication of values and norms to external stakeholders and within the firm. Indeed, for very small firms these kinds of instruments are not really functional. A final reason why large firms will make more use of formal instruments to foster corporate social responsibility is that the competitiveness of the output market of the firm might be stronger for small firms than for large firms. As Graafland (2002c) theoretically shows, the costs involved with a high administrative burden caused by the application of various instruments may be too high for these firms.

Although small firms make less use of the various formal instruments, there are some similarities between large and small enterprises. In particular, like large firms, small firms make relatively good use of a social handbook and a confidential person. Another 11 per cent plan to introduce a social handbook. Another similarity is that an ethics committee, ethical training and commitment to the NEVI code are least popular, whereas codes of conduct and ISO certification take an intermediate position. The most important exception is the position of the member of the board. In contrast to large firms, this is the most common instrument that small firms use to communicate values and norms. Moreover, another 12 per cent of the small firms consider this to be a useful instrument. This confirms the importance of the informal culture that fits the relatively small scale of small firms and facilitates direct communication of values and norms by members of the board.

Interrelationship between different instruments

Table 8.6 presents the relationship between the use of different instruments. In almost all cases there is a significant correlation between all combinations of instruments. However, in only a few cases is this correlation mildly strong (correlation >0.5 and determination coefficient (r^2 >0.25). This indicates that once firms become aware of the importance of using formal instruments to foster the ethical standards within the organisation, they are somewhat more inclined to adopt a combination of various complementary instruments. For example, if a firm introduces a code of conduct that defines the standards in a very compact way, it may also need a social handbook to spell out the more concrete and detailed rules. Furthermore, if the firm takes ethical standards seriously, it must also create procedures for employees to complain about unjust treatment, which requires an ethics committee or confidential person.

Comparison of use of instruments with other research

In order to benchmark the efforts of the firms in the two Dutch provinces North Brabant and Zeeland from an international perspective, we have compared our results with findings from Ulrich *et al.* (1998). They investigated the use of instruments by 550 German and 224 Swiss firms. As their sample only consists of large firms, we only compare their results with the findings for the large firms in our sample.

For the code of conduct and social reporting, our results are very similar to the results of Ulrich *et al.* They find that 29 per cent of the large German and Swiss firms do not know of the code of conduct or do not consider it a useful tool. In our sample, this percentage is only slightly higher, namely 32 per cent. Also with respect to the publication of a social report the results are very similar. In both samples, 23 per cent of the firms do not know about social reporting or do not regard it as useful. Similar findings apply to the ethics committee and ethical training. In the German and Swiss sample 74 per cent did not know of the instrument of an ethics committee or regarded them as not useful (against 77 per cent for our sample). On the other hand, the number of large firms that have such a committee is somewhat larger for Dutch firms (17 per cent against 5 per cent for German firms). Furthermore, 8 per cent of the German and Swiss firms regularly provide ethics training and 5 per cent plan to do so, whereas 68 per cent do not know this instrument or do not regard it as useful. In the Dutch sample, 14 per cent use this instrument but 74 per cent do not know of it or consider it to be irrelevant.

Table 8.6 Bivariate correlation[a]

	Code of conduct	*ISO certification*	*NEVI code*	*Social reporting*	*Social handbook*	*Confidential person*	*Ethics committee*	*Board member*	*Ethical training*
Code of conduct	X	**0.29**	**0.30**	**0.58**	**0.51**	**0.47**	**0.53**	**0.37**	**0.40**
ISO		X	**0.33**	**0.29**	**0.44**	**0.36**	0.17	*0.22*	0.19
NEVI			X	**0.31**	*0.23*	*0.24*	**0.51**	*0.23*	**0.32**
Report				X	**0.60**	**0.49**	**0.42**	*0.23*	**0.32**
Handbook					X	**0.72**	**0.31**	**0.40**	*0.23*
Conf. person						X	**0.38**	**0.55**	0.20
Ethics committee							X	*0.43*	**0.41**
Board member								X	*0.22*
Ethical training									X

[a] Values in **bold** are significant at the 0.01 level; values in ***italics*** are significant at the 0.05 level.

More differences are found for the other instruments. In particular, the Dutch firms in Brabant and Zeeland use confidential persons relatively actively. In German and Swiss firms 50 per cent do not know this instrument and another 18 per cent judge it as irrelevant. For the Dutch firms, these percentages are 2 per cent and 5 per cent respectively. Also the accountability of a board member with respect to ethical issues features higher for Dutch firms than for German and Swiss firms. In the German and Swiss sample, 21 per cent considered this instrument not useful (against 9 per cent in our sample). Moreover, 50 per cent of the German and Swiss firms are unfamiliar with this instrument against 14 per cent in our research.

Unfortunately we cannot compare our results with the study by Ulrich *et al.* for the other instruments – ISO certification, NEVI code and social handbook.

A source for comparison of our results from a national perspective is provided by recent research by the management consultancy KPMG in cooperation with the VNO-NCW North[7] on corporate social responsibility by firms in three northern provinces in the Netherlands.[8] In this research, 43 per cent of the firms in Friesland, Groningen and Drenthe are found to have a code of conduct, which is relatively low compared with the 51 per cent in our sample. However, the situation is changing rapidly. Within three years, 70 per cent of the firms expect to have developed their own code of conduct, which is higher than in our sample.

Second, the research by KPMG shows that 52 per cent of the firms in the three northern provinces of the Netherlands have a confidential person. In this respect, the large firms in North Brabant and Zeeland have a much higher score, namely of 84 per cent.

Concluding, we do not find evidence that large firms in North Brabant and Zeeland differ very much from large German firms or other Dutch firms. They even seem to use certain instruments more actively, such as a confidential person and a responsible board member. However, it should be noted that the relatively low response rate of 15 per cent for large firms in our sample does not permit strong conclusions in this respect.

Interrelationship between strategy and instruments

Table 8.7 describes the use of instruments per type of strategy. As could be expected, firms that have filled in 'no strategy' are indeed least actively using instruments for organising ethics in the firm. This conclusion holds for all instruments (except the NEVI code).

A second finding that fits with an *a priori* hypothesis is that firms that stress the 'compliance strategy' are most actively using instruments that

Table 8.7 Strategy and instruments[a]

	Code	*ISO*	*NEVI*	*Social report*	*Social handbook*	*Confidential person*	*Ethics committee*	*Board member*	*Ethical training*
Compliance	60.0	100.0	18.2	33.3	84.6	76.9	25.0	69.2	25.0
Integrity	22.2	42.3	3.4	34.5	62.1	55.2	3.8	57.1	7.4
Dialogue	59.3	58.1	12.9	59.4	69.7	67.7	18.8	72.7	12.5
No strategy	29.6	30.8	3.8	21.4	39.3	46.4	3.7	51.9	3.7

[a] As a percentage of the respondents.

facilitate the communication of concrete and verifiable rules within the firm, like code of conduct, ISO certification and social handbook. More surprising is that these firms make relatively high use of confidential persons, ethics committees and ethical training. Although the use of confidential person and ethics committee are not inconsistent with the compliance strategy, one would have expected ethical training to be the most popular instrument of firms that favour an integrity strategy.

As expected, firms that favour the dialogue strategy make more use of codes of conduct and social reporting as instruments that facilitate the communication with external stakeholders. They also make relatively high use of a board member who is answerable for ethical issues. This suggests that this instrument can serve the purpose of communicating the commitment of the firm to values and norms to external stakeholders.

Finally, we unexpectedly find that firms that favour an integrity strategy are not as active in using various instruments as firms with a compliance or dialogue strategy. This holds for all instruments.

Multiple regression analysis results

In this section we formally test the hypothesis already indicated by Table 8.5 that large companies make more use of formal instruments to foster CSR. In addition, we use the statistical analysis to research the interrelationship between the use of instruments and other external factors like the sector in which the company operates and whether the company is a family business or non-family business.

Instruments

The results of the regression analysis of the relationship between instruments and exogenous variables are reported in Table 8.8. In Table 8.8 the dependent variable is a dummy that is set at 'one' if the firm uses the particular instrument. Otherwise it is zero. The last column tests for the use of the sum of all instruments.

Table 8.8 Results of multiple regression analysis for instruments[a]

	Code of conduct	*ISO certification*	*NEVI code*	*Social reporting*	*Social handbook*	*Confidential person*	*Ethics committee*	*Board member*	*Ethical training*	*Total*
Number of employees	0.10	0.18	0.07	0.73	0.30	0.26	0.02	0.05	0.02	1.37
	(1.11)	(2.19)	(0.91)	(3.13)	(4.21)	(3.25)	(0.23)	(0.52)	(0.25)	(2.80)
	{0.267}	{0.031}	{0.365}	{0.000}	{0.000}	{0.002}	{0.818}	{0.603}	{0.806}	{0.007}
Subsidiary	0.45	0.12	0.13	0.97	0.17	0.30	0.30	0.11	0.16	1.93
	(4.26)	(1.33)	(1.67)	(3.64)	(2.09)	(3.43)	(3.76)	(1.00)	(1.96)	(3.45)
	{0.000}	{0.188}	{0.098}	{0.001}	{0.039}	{0.001}	{0.000}	{0.316}	{0.053}	{0.001}
Metal manufacturing	0.22	0.22	0.07	0.51	0.13	0.01	0.15	0.02	0.02	1.25
	(2.03)	(2.35)	(0.83)	(1.88)	(1.50)	(0.65)	(1.75)	(0.17)	(0.25)	(2.22)
	{0.045}	{0.021}	{0.411}	{0.262}	{0.137}	{0.515}	{0.084}	{0.867}	{0.806}	{0.030}
Construction	0.15	0.37	0.05	0.83	0.15	0.01	0.00	–0.06	–0.06	1.15
	(1.29)	(3.70)	(0.61)	(2.92)	(1.66)	(0.80)	(0.04)	(0.50)	(0.62)	(1.90)
	{0.201}	{0.000}	{0.541}	{0.018}	{0.099}	{0.425}	{0.972}	{0.622}	{0.540}	{0.062}
Financial services	0.15	–0.19	–0.09	0.04	0.04	0.00	0.07	–0.02	0.05	0.55
	(1.41)	(1.88)	(1.06)	(0.19)	(0.46)	(0.41)	(0.87)	(0.18)	(0.60)	(0.95)
	{0.163}	{0.063}	{0.294}	{0.117}	{0.644}	{0.682}	{0.389}	{0.862}	{0.548}	{0.345}
Family	0.06	0.04	0.13	0.18	–0.06	0.10	0.16	0.05	0.05	0.43
	(0.64)	(0.52)	(1.76)	(0.73)	(0.79)	(1.32)	(2.15)	(0.52)	(0.63)	(0.79)
	{0.523}	{0.601}	{0.082}	{0.624}	{0.434}	{0.191}	{0.035}	{0.602}	{0.532}	{0.431}
Intercept	0.52	0.49	0.16	0.39	0.62	0.64	0.27	0.737	0.267	3.55
	(4.31)	(4.66)	(1.71)	(3.86)	(6.63)	(6.23)	(3.01)	(5.84)	(2.81)	(5.63)
	{0.000}	{0.000}	{0.091}	{0.018}	{0.000}	{0.000}	{0.003}	{0.000}	{0.006}	{0.000}
R^2	0.35	0.37	0.11	0.47	0.38	0.33	0.20	0.03	0.08	0.43
R^2 adj	0.31	0.33	0.05	0.40	0.34	0.29	0.14	–0.04	0.02	0.39
F	7.64	8.59	1.80	11.08	9.78	7.85	3.66	0.42	1.30	9.02

[a] T-values between brackets, p-values between braces.

In most cases the F-test shows that the external factors have a substantial and significant impact on the use of the particular instrument. Only in the case of the NEVI code, responsibility of the board member and ethical training is the F-test well below the critical value. In the case of the NEVI code and ethical training this is probably due to the low use of these instruments (see Table 8.5).

Table 8.8 statistically confirms the outcome in the results section that large firms are more actively using various instruments for organising ethics. For ISO certification, social reporting, social handbook, and confidential person this impact is significant; for the other instruments we find a positive but insignificant impact. Also, being a subsidiary of a larger firm has a positive impact on the use of instruments, notably for a code of conduct, social reporting, social handbook, confidential person and an ethics committee. This may be due to the fact that the local firm can benefit from the provisions offered by the total firm. Another explanation is that firms that have more than one subsidiary have a greater need to communicate and coordinate the ethical standards because of possible cultural differences between the local divisions.

From the sectoral perspective, we find that metal manufacturing and construction firms are more actively using ISO certification, social reporting and a social handbook than the financial service sector and the retail sector. This fits with the character of the production processes in the metal manufacturing sector and the construction sector. One would expect that the financial sector might be especially interested in communication with external stakeholders by codes of conduct and social reporting. In addition, because of the larger share of women working in the financial sector, confidential persons and ethics committees may be more common because of the higher probability of sexual harassment. However, the estimation results only weakly support these effects.

In terms of the relationship between family business and use of instrument, the effects are in most cases insignificant. On average, being a family firm has a small positive impact on the use of instruments. Only in the case of the use of an ethics committee is the impact significant.

Conclusions

This chapter investigates the use of various strategies and instruments to organise ethics by large and small firms in two provinces in the Netherlands. We find that:

- Large firms make relatively more use of an integrity strategy that defines core values without controlling or sanctioning mechanisms. Small firms rely relatively more on a dialogue strategy in which they try to learn from stakeholders which aspects of corporate social responsibility are most important to realise. The compliance strategy that communicates fixed standards, controls the behaviour of the workers and applies sanctions in case of infringements, is least popular both among large and small enterprises. This seems to fit the Dutch consensus culture.
- Firms that favour a compliance strategy make relatively high use of a code of conduct, ISO certification and social handbook, whereas firms that favour a dialogue strategy are most active in social reporting and assigning a board member who is particularly answerable for ethical questions. Firms that have no clear strategy least actively use formal instruments to organise ethical standards in the firm.
- In many cases the use of one particular instrument to foster ethical behaviour of the firm is significantly positively correlated to the use of another particular instrument. For example, firms that have a social handbook also often make use of a confidential person.
- Large firms make relatively more use of several formal instruments to foster ethical behaviour. The most popular instruments are, respectively, social handbook, confidential person and ISO9001/14001 certification. Furthermore, a significant proportion (more than half) of the large firms also make use of a code of conduct, publication of an annual social report and a member of the board who is clearly responsible for ethical questions. Only a small percentage of the large firms has an ethics committee or provides ethical training to the employees.
- Small firms make relatively little use of these instruments compared with large firms. The most common instrument to communicate values and norms within small firms is that a member of the board is answerable for ethical questions. This confirms the importance of an informal culture for small firms.
- For all instruments distinguished in the research (code of conduct, ISO certification, signing of NEVI code, social reporting, social handbook, confidential person, ethics committee, board member responsible for ethical issues and ethical training) we find that subsidiaries of a larger firm more actively use the particular instrument than do independent firms. This finding also holds for larger firms and stresses the value of these instruments as a means to coordinate the ethical standards between different subsidiaries within a large firm. 

- Firms in the metal manufacturing sector more actively use codes of conduct, ISO certification, social reporting, social handbook and ethics committee than firms in the financial services sector or retail sector. Firms in the construction sector are relatively most active in using ISO certification, social reporting and social handbook.
- Family firms and non-family firms show very similar patterns. Only in the case of the ethics committee does being a family firm have a significant positive impact on the use of the instrument.

If we look at these research findings it becomes clear that large firms are implementing and developing a quite complete set of instruments to organise their efforts with respect to their social responsibility. In this respect there are no spectacular differences with large firms in the northern part of the Netherlands, nor with large firms in Germany and Switzerland. Therefore, there seems to be no further need for initiatives that stimulate the use of instruments by large firms in the southern part of the Netherlands. However, since this study did not evaluate the way these instruments are used, further research is needed to determine the professional level at which these instruments are developed and implemented. If 62 per cent of the large firms claim to have an annual social report, one might become curious about the quality of these reports. Sometimes a social report means no more than a statement by a member of the board of directors about improvement of working conditions. In general, more research should be done on the quality and effectiveness of the instruments that are being used to improve social responsibility of large firms. Such research should encompass the views of stakeholders too.

With respect to small firms it still makes sense to foster awareness of the instruments for organising CSR among entrepreneurs and managers, since many of them have indicated that they are not familiar with such important instruments like a code of conduct, social handbook and ethical training. At the same time the research findings (Table 8.5) indicate that a lot of instruments are known but rejected or rejected at first glance. The usual instruments for organising social responsibility have no appeal to a large group of small firms. This brings us to the question of whether there is a viable alternative to the standard way of organising CSR. The popularity of the dialogue strategy combined with the measure of making a member of the board answerable for ethical issues points us in the direction of ethical leadership and the importance of a climate of mutual trust between the firm and its stakeholders. Every business needs mutual trust to function properly, otherwise its transaction costs would be too high or it would have to choose the immoral strategy of hit and run (Etzioni, 1988). Formal instruments like a code of ethics and a social report can be used to induce trust in situations where there is no strong personal tie between the board of directors and a stakeholder. In the case of small firms, personal ties are probably much more important, especially the trustworthiness of the owner-manager of the firm. It can be a relative advantage to a small firm if the climate of trust is based on relatively strong personal ties instead of on impersonal instruments like a code of ethics that could give stakeholders an impression of the corporate identity and trustworthiness of a large firm. For instance, if something goes wrong, one does not have to follow all kinds of formal procedures to inform the firm about the problem. A simple call to the owner-manager of the firm should be enough to get the attention needed. We suspect that the dialogue strategy in the case of small firms does not amount to much more than this reliance on approachability. Its simplicity is perhaps its greatest strength, because in the end every dissatisfied stakeholder wants to speak to the boss in person. Our study does not allow us to confirm these assumptions, but we would recommend further research into this matter. Research could be done on the motives of small firms that reject most instruments for organising CSR and on how they deal with complaints and expectations of their stakeholders. Only then we can answer the question whether there is a viable alternative to organising CSR with the well-known instruments discussed in this chapter.

Notes

1. This chapter was first published as the following article: Graafland, J., B. van de Ven and N. Stoffele, 'Strategies and Instruments for Organising CSR by Small and Large Businesses in the Netherlands', *Journal of Business Ethics*, 47(1), (2003), 45–60. With kind permission from Kluwer Academic Publishers.
2. However, other research cannot detect any positive influence of a written code of conduct on ethical behaviour or perceptions. See, for example, Kohut and Corriher (1994) and Marnburg (2000).
3. See, for more information on the ISO (International Standards Organisation) norms: www.iso.ch
4. Another example is the international Social Accountability 8000, developed by the American Council on Economic Priorities Accreditation Agency (CEPAA) in cooperation with employers, unions and non-governmental organisations (NGOs). SA8000 mainly concerns labour aspects. Since our research focuses on Dutch firms operating in local markets, we do not include this certification in our questionnaire.
5. The reason for the selection of these two provinces is that two regional employer organisations and one employee organisation in these provinces financed the research.

6. This distinction between small and large firms means that we do not follow the distinction between small and medium sized firms as is common in research that focuses on small and medium sized firms. The reason for this is that we believe that for our research objective a rather rough distinction between small and large firms suffices.
7. This name (VNO-NCW) is a result of a fusion between the Dutch Association of Enterprises (VNO: Verbond van Nederlandse Ondernemingen), and the Dutch Christian Union of Employers (NCW: Nederlands Christelijk Werkgeversverbond).
8. KPMG, VNO-NCW, Kamers van Koophandel (Chambers of Commerce) Friesland, Groningen and Drenthe, 2002, 'Maatschappelijk Ondernemen is Core Business', Brochure.

References

Adams, J.S., A. Tashchian and T.H. Shore, 'Codes of Ethics as Signals for Ethical Behavior', *Journal of Business Ethics*, 29, (2001) 199–211.

Etzioni, A., *The Moral Dimension. Towards a New Economics* (New York: The Free Press, 1988).

Graafland, J.J., 'Profits and Principles: Four Perspectives', *Journal of Business Ethics*, 35, (2002a) 293–305.

Graafland, J.J., 'Sourcing Ethics in the Textile Sector: The Case of C&A', *Business Ethics: A European Review*, 11(3), July, (2002b) 282–94.

Graafland, J.J., 'Modelling the Trade Off Between Profits and Principles', *De Economist*, 150, (2002c) 129–54.

Graafland, J.J., B.W. van de Ven and N.C.G.M. Stoffele, 'Wat betekent maatschappelijk ondernemen concreet?', Tilburg University, (2002) www.uvt.nl/fww/cmo

Hummels, H. and E. Karssing, 'Ethiek organizeren', in R. Jeurissen (ed.), *Bedrijfsethiek een goede zaak* (Assen: Van Gorcum, 2000) pp. 196–224.

Kaptein, M. and J. Wempe, 'Twelve Gordian Knots When Developing an Organizational Code of Ethics', *Journal of Business Ethics*, 17, (1998) 853–69.

Kaptein, M. and F. Buiter, *De integere organizatie 2* (The Hague: Stichting Beroepsmoraal en Misdaadpreventie, 2001).

Kohut, G.E. and S.E. Corriher, 'The Relationship of Age, Gender, Experience and Awareness of Written Ethics Policies to Business Decision Making', *SAM Advanced Management Journal*, Winter, (1994) 32–9.

Marnburg, E., 'The Behavioural Effects of Corporate Ethical Codes: Empirical Findings and Discussion', *Business Ethics: A European Review*, 9(3), (2000) 200–10.

McIntosh, M., D. Leipziger, K. Jones and G. Coleman, *Corporate Citizenship. Successful Strategies for Responsible Companies* (London: Pitman Publishing, 1998).

Sharp Paine, L., 'Managing for Organizational Integrity', *Harvard Business Review*, 72, (1994) 106–17.

Sociaal Economische Raad (SER), *Corporate Social Responsibility* (Assen: Van Gorcum, 2001).

Spence, L.J., R. Jeurissen and R. Rutherfoord, 'Small Business and the Environment in the UK and the Netherlands: Towards Stakeholder Cooperation', *Business Ethics Quarterly*, 10(4), (2000) 945–65.

Trevino, Linda K. and K.A. Nelson, *Managing Business Ethics. Straight Talk About How To Do It Right* (New York: John Wiley & Sons, 1999).

Ulrich, P., Y. Lunau and T. Weber, 'Ethikmassnahmen in der Unternehmenspraxis', in P. Ulrich and J. Wieland (eds), *Unterhehmensethik in der Praxis. Impulse aus den USA, Deutschland und der Schweiz*, (Bern: Verlag Paul Haupt) (1998) pp. 121–94.

Van de Ven, B.W., 'Strategische Freiheit, kommunikative Rationalität und moralische Verantwortung des Unternehmens', in H.G. Nutzinger und das Berliner Forum zur Wirtschafts- und Unternehmensethik (eds), *Wirtschafts- und Unternehmensethik: Kritik einer neuen Generation* (Munich and Mering: Rainer Hampp Verlag, 1999).

9

Aristotle in Your Local Garage: Enlarging Social Capital with an Ethics Test

Lutz Preuss

In this chapter it is argued that a fuzziness in defining social capital (as mentioned in Chapter 1) is problematic in considering its usefulness as a concept. In particular, the paucity regarding the conceptualisation of an ethical perspective in social capital is identified.

Social capital is becoming an increasingly popular concept in numerous social science fields. Emerging from sociology and political science, it has been applied as a useful heuristic device for drawing attention to cultural factors and context-dependent resources in social life in subjects as diverse as education, criminology, architecture, medicine, regional regeneration, third world development and last but not least economics and management studies. Scholars have even suggested that social capital theory may be 'close to becoming a joint concept for all social sciences' (Paldam 2000, p. 631).

Such diversity of application has led to an array of diverging definitions. As one of the earlier authors, Bourdieu (1985, p. 248) defines social capital as the 'aggregate of the actual or potential resources which are linked to possession of a durable network of more or less institutionalized relationships of mutual acquaintance or recognition'. For Fukuyama (2001, p. 7) it is 'an instantiated informal norm that promotes co-operation between two or more individuals'. Narayan and Pritchett (1999) define social capital as the quantity and quality of membership in voluntary associations and the related social norms, while Habisch (1999) defines it as the set of relationships, both formal and informal ones, that allows a society to permanently overcome social interaction problems and thus reap the benefits of social cooperation. Portes (1998, p. 6) sees a definitory consensus emerging in that 'social capital stands for the ability of actors to secure benefits by virtue of membership in social networks or other social structures', yet it does remain a fuzzy concept.

The vagueness of the definitions is compounded by the equally multifaceted nature of its manifestations (Putnam and Goss, 2001). Social capital may be formal or informal, depending on whether group members meet in an organised fashion or just spontaneously. It may differ in the degree of density, where high density is characterised by membership in overlapping organisations. In a high-density context, largely the same individuals meet at work, on social occasions and in religious services. There are internally and externally focused forms of social capital, which either aim to represent primarily the aims of their members or those of the larger society. This links to bridging and bonding forms of social capital, where the former brings together individuals from different backgrounds, while the aim of the latter is to bind together people that are similar in important criteria, such as ethnic background, class, education or age.

Fuzziness also emerges in the relationship between social capital and neighbouring concepts, such as trust. Where Fukuyama (1995) in his distinction between high and low trust societies more or less equates trust with social capital, Putnam (2000) sees it as a quantitative indicator of social capital, while for Coleman (1988) trustworthiness is a precondition for social capital. Such ambiguity leads to the criticism that social capital is merely an 'umbrella concept' (Hirsch and Levin, 1999) for concepts like trust, organisational culture, social networks, organisational embeddedness and others.

There is, furthermore, debate about whether social capital is indeed a form of capital (Coleman, 1988; Portes, 1998; Edwards and Foley, 1998; Habisch, 1999). On the affirmative side, it is a long-lived asset into which resources can be invested with the expectation of some future return. Social, like other forms of capital, can be appropriated by individual or collective agents and can be converted into other forms of benefits, such as economic gain. Thus social capital can substitute or complement other resources. However, in contrast to other forms of capital, social capital resides in the relationship, not in an individual person, and has an unspecified time-scale. It needs regular maintenance, which contrasts with financial capital (even if not with human or physical capital). In contrast to physical capital, social capital does not depreciate with use. Yet it can be destroyed unilaterally by one actor in a dyadic relation withdrawing their support, a scenario which contrasts with the other forms of capital. Social capital is of a more limited mobility than traditional forms of capital. Thus the neoclassical assumption that factors of

production spontaneously even out between regions is not met by social capital.

An ethics extension for social capital

One of the reasons for this definitory vagueness, it is argued here, lies in the under-conceptualisation of the link between social capital and moral philosophy. Social capital has an inherent ethical dimension, yet ethics is hardly ever specifically referred to by authors on the subject. The importance of the ethical dimension is strengthened by a gradual – and largely unacknowledged – drift to a normative conceptualisation (Edwards and Foley, 1998; Portes 1998). It is especially Putnam (1993 and 2000) who applies a normative perspective in his ambitious project to re-create by 2010 the social capital levels the United States had in the 1960s. Within the World Bank the social capital concept has similarly shot to fame as a factor that is critical for the alleviation of poverty in developing countries.[1] In management, a normative perspective has been propagated by authors such as Cohen and Prusak (2001) or Anand, Glick and Manz (2002, p. 88). In today's environment of increasingly global competition, the latter maintain, organisational advantage is rarely derived from superior technologies or value-added activities of the supply-chain. Rather, firms must increasingly apply knowledge, especially knowledge obtained from outsiders, and 'Social capital is a primary means through which organizations import external knowledge into the firm.'

A large number of other authors, even if they do not directly propagate a normative perspective, write in a 'frequently celebratory tone' and use the concept 'as shorthand for the positive consequences of sociability' (Portes, 1998, p. 2f.). Thus social cohesion in a neighbourhood is linked to reduced violence (Sampson, Raudenbush and Earls, 1997). In rural Tanzania, household members in villages that display an overall higher level of social capital are more likely to enjoy better public services and use more advanced agricultural methods (Narayan and Pritchett, 1999). Religious schools in the US benefit from a tighter network of shared beliefs among pupils, teachers and parents, which allows pupils to perform better than those at other schools (Coleman, 1988). The accumulation of social capital is as crucial for architects in acquiring new projects (Skaates, Tikkanen and Alajoutsijärvi, 2002) as it is for a reduced mortality risk and a better state of mental health (Seeman, 1996). In the propagation of these beneficial tendencies, a deeper ontological debate looms. Social capital seemingly reflects soft post-material values in contrast to the 'old capitals', which stand for material values. 'Social capital might be

seen as the "revenge" of the "soft" social sciences against the "hardness" of economics' (Paldam, 2000, p. 634), as a backlash against the invasion of economic concepts into the 'softer' social sciences.

This is not to argue that authors on social capital are unaware that network-based outcomes can have both positive and negative aspects (see especially Leenders and Gabbay, 1999). From a sociological perspective, Portes (1998) sees several positive consequences of social capital. The social capital created in tightly knit communities can help parents, teachers and law enforcement agencies in establishing and maintaining social control. Social capital can also be a source of family support, for example in the education of children. The most common function of social capital, however, lies in its ability to provide network-mediated benefits beyond the immediate family. On the dark side, social capital can, by privileging group members, restrict access to opportunities for outsiders. Group membership can require conformity, which may lead to restrictions on individual freedom. Group members can make excessive claims on more successful or entrepreneurial members and thus thwart their development. Groups may also keep the more ambitious members back, leading to a downward levelling of norms.

Within the concept of social capital there is no way to measure whether an application of social capital is beneficial to the individual and their society or otherwise. For example, Coleman (1988) cites as an example of social capital the study circles of South Korean radical students, who hailed from the same towns, attended the same schools and are members of the same religious congregations. These links provided the social relations that aided the move from individual protest to organised revolt in South Korea. Coleman himself draws a parallel with Lenin's call for workers' cells in Tsarist Russia. One could object that in the Russian example it was precisely the clandestine nature of these cells that distorted working-class politics from social democracy into Stalinist oppression. The argument becomes clearer when the South Korean students are compared to a third manifestation of social capital: terrorist networks like IRA, ETA or Al Qaeda. All of these utilise the same close personal links derived from living in the same neighbourhoods and attending the same religious institutions. Yet social capital theory does not provide an instrument to explain why one might see the first manifestation of social capital as beneficial for society, have mixed feelings about the second one and reject the third.

This observation highlights another drawback of social capital, the difficulty in measuring it (Knack and Keefer, 1997). One of the most widely used measurements of social capital is Putnam's instrument, which establishes membership in voluntary organisations in a region. While applicable to politics and sociology, the instrument is less relevant to a number of other fields, including business studies. Furthermore, ambiguity resides in the definition of a voluntary organisation, as there is considerable overlap between voluntary organisations, business and the state. Putnam's instrument also neglects the intensity of contact between members of a voluntary organisation. More important for the argument presented here is a suggested benignness weighting (Paldam, 2000), where non-benign voluntary organisations should receive a negative weight when the social capital in an area is calculated. However, even if benign and malign social capital in an area could be calculated, the bigger problem resides in evaluating a manifestation of social capital as either malign or benign, and this cannot be achieved by social capital theory.

In addition to evaluating manifestations of social capital, there also seems to be no mechanism within the concept of social capital to *a priori* determine the amount of investment that is exactly right in any given case. Since investment into social capital can easily overshoot or fall short of the right amount, this is a serious drawback for individuals who want to plan their investment into social and other forms of capital. It similarly brings difficulties for public policy-makers who aim to create an optimum level of social capital and associated gains in their region or country. We have thus arrived at conceptual fuzziness, combined with an inability to give advice to business practitioners and policy-makers in concrete situations and a danger of our concept being applicable to marginal scenarios only.

However, the direction in which social capital theory is seemingly heading is already mapped by ethics, the aim of which is to establish rules for the good life and, transferred to collectives of individuals, to establish rules for good organisations. Thus the suggestion here is to make the often implicit reference to ethics in the social capital debate

an explicit one and to enlarge the concept of social capital with an ethics test. Such an ethics test would have to examine, first, whether it is ethical for an individual to leverage his or her social capital in a specific situation. Since social capital is usually defined as a collective problem-solving instrument, the ethics test also needs to be applied at the societal level. Second, the question needs to be asked whether the use of social capital in any given situation is good for the society to which the individual

belongs. Hence one should speak of valuable social capital only where the ethics twin test is met (or at least clearly mark cases where network-mediated benefits are accrued with consequences that fall foul of the tests as 'negative social capital').

One strand of ethical theory that can play this role is virtue ethics, which goes back to the philosophical writings of Aristotle. Aristotelian virtue ethics emphasises the importance of a person's character for morality. He suggests that the highest human good is happiness, not in a crude sense but in a comprehensive sense, which carries notions of flourishing and wellbeing. This highest good is closely linked to the function of a human being, which is to obey reason, as this is the main criterion to set humans apart from other species. As a good flautist plays the flute well or a good knife cuts well, Aristotle argues, so a good human is good at applying reason. Acting in accordance with good reason is the distinguishing feature of moral behaviour. Reason helps to avoid both excess and deficiency; for example the virtue of courage is the healthy mean between the vices of cowardice and rashness. To acquire this kind of virtue, humans need practical wisdom, which can only be acquired by experience and habituation. Thus Aristotle (1985, pp. 20–4) defines that 'the virtue of a human being will . . . be the state that makes a human being good and makes him perform his function well'. Virtue ethics can also address Portes's (1998) question as to what motivates 'donors' of social capital to help others; his two categories of instrumental and 'consummatory' motives are hereby combined into one single analytical category.

It is noticeable that notions of ethics and morality are, if not absent, then at least of a marginal role in the social capital debate. One exception is the observation by Habisch (1999) that social capital can be built or accumulated where acting in accordance with moral norms – which are shaped by institutional arrangements and personal experiences – turns out to be advantageous in the longer run. The scores for individual pairs of agents do not necessarily have to balance out, as long as each actor has the safe knowledge that a favour granted to one person will eventually be repaid by someone else. Systems of moral values that do not pay off in the longer term get eroded in learning and adaptation processes. While these arguments discuss the role of morality in the building of social capital, they do not go beyond explaining this one element of its foundations.

Enlarging social capital with an ethics test links well to the conventional use of capital. A characteristic of capital is that an expenditure produces beneficial outcomes. Investment in a machine that is not fit for the intended purpose does not constitute physical capital. A person might strive hard to acquire knowledge, but if she cannot make use of it (her society might, for example, not appreciate having additional archaeologists) then her acquired knowledge does not constitute human capital. This is quite opposite to the argument presented by Putnam and Goss (2001, p. 23), who suggest that a nuclear power plant still represents a large sum of physical capital, even if it emits radiation and hence a negative externality for society. Certainly, the nuclear power plant requires capital to be erected and constitutes an asset while it produces energy, but when social pressures begin to demand the imposition of safety features, the book value of the plant declines in proportion. If it were to close completely, it no longer represents capital, beyond that which may be salvaged by selling machinery or property. Bad debt does not constitute capital. Similarly, activities where network-derived consequences are negative fail the ethics test. It is argued that these do not constitute social capital either.

Applying the enlarged social capital theory to business

The importance of the ethics twin test will in the following be illustrated by applying social capital theory to business, especially to small and medium sized companies. An example of social capital in business is a garage owner who engages in maintaining friendly relations with competitors because all the necessary tools are not owned, or for some reason the owner-manager prefers not to undertake a particular task. Good relations with other garage owners enable work to be taken on anyway, knowing that competitors can in all likelihood be relied upon to help out. Another example is a proprietor of an ethnic minority business, who provides employment to members of his or her own ethnicity. The interaction with competitors and community members leads the participants to redefine their relationships to each other. The ongoing relationship may lead to justified expectations of the other side, and thus social capital emerges. The garage owner helps out competitors, knowing that when he is in need of support they would help him too. The minority-business owner provides employment for other members of the ethnic group, and in turn can benefit from a labour force whose qualifications, skills and work ethos are familiar.

The use of concepts borrowed from economics leads to a search for answers from economic sources. In other words, a discourse involving capital cannot avoid implying related economic concepts, such as opportunity cost. Advice for the garage owner would have to take into account alternative targets for the time, effort and money spent on relationship building, for example investing into marketing or superior technology. Where such alternative investment yields a higher return, the garage owner would have to be advised to stop investing into bonds with competitors in his local community. The solidarity effect, which builds up with social capital, may also over-embed the actor, reduce the flow of new information into the network and result in parochialism and inertia. Applying Aristotelian theory to the garage owner, virtue ethics requires him to take responsibility for his own development, the business' and that of the employees. Virtue ethics can thus point to the mean between investing too much or too little in social capital and in both cases risking the continued existence of the business. In the ethnic minority case, the tightly knit communities may create free-rider problems or unrealistically high expectations of how many jobs the firm can provide. Virtue ethics shows the mean between helping members of one's ethnic group and thereby building oneself a better image in the community and the downside of becoming too embedded in one's own ethnic group and, for example, foregoing the benefits of a potentially wider skills group.

From a broader societal perspective, the garage owner case highlights the fine line between cooperation and restricting competition. In the age of information and globalisation, cooperation across companies becomes an important source of information and need not lead to a restriction of competition (Habisch, 1999; Fukuyama, 2001; Anand, Glick and Manz, 2002). For example, an industry association can apply such cooperation to establish improved environmental standards, as the Responsible Care initiative in the chemical industry did. On the other hand, it is possible that the tool-sharing activities of the small garage owner-manager might lead to a suboptimal use of resources in comparison with larger garage companies. Where this leads to higher costs for the customer, it would be a case of social capital being used to evade the market, the aim of which is after all to limit producer cooperation where it would lead to the detriment of the customer. Applying Aristotle to the societal level, virtue ethics points to the mean between restricted competition and possibly higher prices to the consumer on the one hand and the benefits of the continued existence of the small business on the other.

The ethnic minority case similarly highlights issues that can become questionable, when seen from the point of view of the wider society. Preference for one ethnic group may be acceptable in small companies, where it can reduce recruitment costs, yet it is nonetheless a form of nepotism and automatically works to the exclusion of other groups. Employing only members of one's own ethnicity can give the owner a greater degree of control over the workforce, who might be less likely to take up their legal rights and succumb to working longer hours than they would in the absence of the strong ties. At a social level, virtue ethics thus establishes the mean between support for one's own ethnic

group on the one hand, and on the other the potential exclusion of other groups as well as the abuse of the ties in exploiting the workforce. The case of nepotism among firms sharing ethnic, religious and social ties is also a counter-example to Habisch's (1999) claim that social capital within religious communities is less problematic than that of business interest groups.

In line with the increasing application of social capital theory in a normative sense, the virtue ethics extension is able to offer normative advice to business people and policy-makers. The first test allows an individual to establish where a person should stop investing in social capital and invest in alternative forms of capital instead. The second test allows an economic policy-maker to assess the outcomes of the current incentive structure for the generation and application of social capital, including an imperative to change the incentive structure if it were found not to be conducive to the public good. The latter is especially important if social capital is to play the role as a link between economic activity and democracy, which Habisch (1999) suggests. As argued above, both tasks cannot be undertaken within the concept of social capital; they can only be accomplished by moral philosophy.

Conclusions

This chapter has argued that social capital has an inherent moral quality, which is reflected in the fact that some authors propagate an explicit normative conceptualisation. It is therefore surprising that references to moral philosophy are virtually non-existent in the literature. This underexposure of the link to moral philosophy may be one of the reasons why a generally accepted definition of the concept has not yet been achieved.

It is suggested here that the implicit reference to ethics should be made an explicit one. Moral philosophy is needed not only for the evaluation of social capital manifestations but also because the concept is unable to determine *a priori* what amount of investment is the right amount. It could not only lead to an allocation that is perceived as being unsocial but also runs the risk of being applicable to ideal-case scenarios only. To avoid these shortfalls, the suggestion is to supplement social capital with an ethical test, which on the basis of Aristotelian virtue ethics asks whether the use of social capital in any given situation promotes the wellbeing and flourishing of the unit under study. This ethics test can be applied to several levels of analysis, of which two are essential: the level of the individual and the society in which the individual is embedded.

At the level of the individual person, virtue ethics can establish whether the application of social capital in a given situation furthers the flourishing of a person, such as an owner of a small or medium sized enterprise. At the level of the local community in which the business and its owner are embedded, virtue ethics can establish how much involvement in local affairs can be demanded of a small and medium sized business before the business or the community begin to suffer. An ethics extension to social capital can also give advice for public policymakers regarding the suitability of the current incentive structure for the generation and use of social capital. If the analysis leads to the evaluation that there is too little (or too much) social capital, the policymaker can undertake the respective changes to the incentive structure. This connection is the more important as social capital can be seen as a link between democracy and the economic sphere.

Social capital theory fulfils several of the features that Hirsch and Levin (1999) discuss as typical of 'umbrella constructs'. The more a field lacks a theoretical consensus, the more it will rely on umbrella constructs to bring together the diverse research elements. The umbrella construct that seeks to tie different research elements together will, however, be eventually challenged in terms of its validity. This process is driven by a dialectic between researchers with a broad perspective, the 'umbrella advocates', and those with a narrower one, the 'validity police'. Thus Hirsch and Levin suggest that an umbrella construct goes through four typical stages: emerging excitement, the validity challenge, tidying up by establishing typologies, and construct collapse. Social capital has clearly been through the emerging excitement phase, but will it survive the validity challenge? It is hoped that the integration of the ethics twin test will strengthen the construct, so that a construct collapse can be avoided.

Note

1. For further details, see the World Bank website: www.worldbank.org/poverty/scapital/index.htm

References

Anand, V., W. H. Glick and C. C. Manz, 'Thriving on the Knowledge of Outsiders: Tapping Organizational Social Capital', *Academy of Management Executive*, 16: 1, (2002) 87–101.

Aristotle, *Nicomachean Ethics*, transl. Terence Irwin (Indianapolis: Hackett Publishing, 1985).

Bourdieu, P., 'The Forms of Capital', in J.G. Richardson (ed.), *Handbook of Theory and Research for the Sociology of Education* (New York: Greenwood, 1985).

Cohen, D. and L. Prusak, 'How to Invest in Social Capital', *Harvard Business Review*, June, (2001) 86–93.

Coleman, J., 'Social Capital in the Creation of Human Capital', *American Journal of Sociology*, 94 (supplement), (1988) 95–120.

Edwards, B. and M.W. Foley, 'Civil Society and Social Capital Beyond Putnam', *American Behavioral Scientist*, 42(1), (1998) 124–39.

Fukuyama, F., *Trust: The Social Virtues and the Creation of Prosperity* (London: Hamish Hamilton, 1995).

Fukuyama, F., 'Social Capital, Civil Society and Development', *Third World Quarterly*, 22(1), (2001) 7–20.

Habisch, A., 'Sozialkapital', in W. Korff (ed.), *Handbuch der Wirtschaftsethik*, Band 4 (Gütersloh: Gütersloher Verlaghaus, 1999), pp. 472–509.

Hirsch, P.M. and D.Z. Levin, 'Umbrella Advocates versus Validity Police: A Life-Cycle Model', *Organization Science: A Journal of the Institute of Management Sciences*, 10(2), (1999) 199–212.

Knack, S. and P. Keefer, 'Does Social Capital Have an Economic Payoff? A Cross-Country Investigation', *Quarterly Journal of Economics*, 112(4), (1997) 1251–88.

Leenders, R.T. and S.M. Gabbay, *Corporate Social Capital and Liability* (Boston: Kluwer Academic Publishers, 1999).

Narayan, D. and L. Pritchett, 'Cents and Sociability: Household Income and Social Capital in Rural Tanzania', *Economic Development & Cultural Change*, 47(4), (1999) 871–97.

Paldam, M, 'Social Capital: Definition and Measurement', *Journal of Economic Surveys*, 14(5), (2000) 629–51.

Portes, A., 'Social Capital: Its Origins and Applications in Modern Sociology', *Annual Review of Sociology*, 24, (1998) 1–24.

Putnam, R., *Making Democracy Work: Civic Traditions in Modern Italy* (Princeton: Princeton University Press, 1993).

Putnam, R., *Bowling Alone: The Collapse and Revival of American Community*, (New York: Simon & Schuster, 2000).

Putnam, R. and K. Goss, 'Einleitung', in R. Putman (ed.), *Gesellschaft und Gemeinsinn – Sozialkapital im internationalen Vergleich* (Gütersloh: Verlag Bertelsmann Stiftung, 2001) pp.15–43.

Sampson, R.J., S.W. Raudenbush and F. Earls, 'Neighborhoods and Violent Crime: A Multilevel Study of Collective Efficacy', *Science*, 227, (1997) 918–24.

Seeman, T.E., 'Social Ties and Health: The Benefits of Social Integration', *Annals of Epidemiology*, 6(5), (1996) 442–51.

Skaates, M.A., H. Tikkanen and K. Alajoutsijärvi, 'Social and Cultural Capital in Project Marketing Service Firms: Danish Architectural Firms on the German Market', *Scandinavian Journal of Management*, 18(4), (2002) 589–609.

10
The Social World of SMEs: The Way Forward

Keith Dickson, André Habisch, René Schmidpeter, Laura J. Spence and Andrea Werner

Policy-makers across Europe seem set on encouraging socially responsible activity by SMEs. If this is the case, there is urgent need for more focused research on what it is that enables and encourages social engagement by SMEs and how this can be supported. However, the findings in this book suggest that this is not a simple formulaic problem-solving phenomenon. Rather, what is needed is an improved understanding of the social world of SMEs, with input from sociology, history, philosophy, economics, regional studies, comparative studies and management studies. In short, there is much more to be done before we fully understand the social world of the SME.

All of the research presented here recognises that SMEs are often already actively engaged in social and community issues and always have been. This needs to be acknowledged clearly. It is the overwhelming common finding of the studies included in this book. This has important implications for future research, especially where comparisons are made with large firms where things may not be so clear-cut, and for policy-makers. Other common findings are noted in the following discussion of the future research and policy agenda for SMEs and social issues.

Future research agenda

In compiling this book we have identified the following areas as being pertinent for future research on social issues and SMEs: refining definitions, better understanding sector differences, clarifying regional and national variations, and researching beyond the reporting of the owner-manager to include all other stakeholders.

Definitions

A number of definitional issues are recurrent throughout this book. They relate to the inconsistencies in defining what a small and medium sized enterprise (SME) is, and the meaning of social responsibility and all the related terms.

This book illustrates the inconsistencies in defining what constitutes a small or medium sized enterprise. Chapter 3, by Spence and Rutherfoord, the first empirical chapter in the book, highlights the basic conundrum in that it only refers to 'small' firms, defined as those being independent, owner-managed and with fewer than 50 employees, whereas the other chapters deal with small *and* medium sized firms. The distinction between small sized firms and medium sized firms is generally passed over without comment by commentators on SMEs. It seems likely, however, that at the extremes there could be significant differences in the practices of a firm with 10 employees (small according to European Union guidelines), and one with 230 (medium according to EU guidelines) (see Appendix A.1 for a summary of the EU guidelines). A medium sized firm is unlikely to be operated along the informal lines of communication and control familiar to the small firm. Furthermore, a medium firm is likely to have departments and devolved responsibility that would be uncommon in the small organisation where the owner-manager maintains an overview of the whole firm. Future research should accommodate an understanding of any distinction between 'small' and 'medium' in a more systematic manner than has been included in this book.

Of the empirically based chapters that deal with SMEs as a collective group, those which include UK studies (Chapter 4 by Schmidpeter and Spence, Chapter 5 by Janjuha-Jivraj and Chapter 6 by Southwell) adopt a broad European Union definition of fewer than 250 employees when identifying SMEs. This may be because the UK's Department of Trade and Industry also follows the EU definitions. Here at least, then, there is some consistency. In Chapter 7 by Maaß and Chapter 8 by Graafland *et al.*, definitions influenced by national institutions in Germany and the Netherlands respectively are adopted. Maaß considers firms with up to 499 employees to be the critical definition of an SME in Germany. Graafland *et al.* adopt the perspective advocated by the organisation for small and medium sized business in the Netherlands, which is fewer than 100 employees. It is unclear to what extent these differing definitions of SME are problematic. It could perhaps be argued that the firms in the research data all avoid being 'large' firms, and that as such they have collective features reflecting the idiosyncrasies of a smaller firm noted in the introduction to the book, i.e. that they are independent and owner-managed, stretched by a broad range of tasks, have limited cash flow, experience survival challenges, are built on personal relationships, are mistrustful of bureaucracy and controlled by informal mechanisms. However, there is certainly room for further clarification and consideration of what is meant by an SME if meaningful comparisons are to be made between research studies.

Other definitional challenges are around the terms used for consideration of social and ethical issues. For the purposes of this book, we have taken very loose definitions and used the umbrella perspective of the 'social world of SMEs' as a catch-all. Some closer work needs to be done on the definitions of the key terms used: social capital, (corporate) social responsibility, corporate citizenship, civic engagement, business ethics. These terms have all been used in this book in a manner which simply conveys a positive moral perspective of social actions taken (generally) outside of the strictly commercial aspects of a business. We would like to see these terms either defined more clearly (and those definitions shared by protagonists) or an open acceptance that the terms are broadly interchangeable and it is down to personal taste which one is chosen.

Social capital has been the most extensively discussed term, in particular in Chapter 1 by Werner and Spence and in closer detail in Chapter 2 by Habisch. A focus has been made primarily on the benefits accrued as a result of social connections. This has resulted in a lack of consideration of possible disbenefits, i.e. the dark side of social capital, and this needs further investigation. In the empirical Chapters 4 (Schmidpeter and Spence) and 5 (Janjuha-Jivraj), social capital was accepted as a basically instrumental perspective without interrogating its moral foundations or considering whether the motives for investing in social capital matter. Chapter 9 by Preuss offers a welcome critique of the social capital concept, highlighting its lack of ethical underpinnings and offering virtue theory as a possible approach to rectify this. More work is needed on the theoretical perspective of social capital relevant to responsibility and SMEs.

Similarly, corporate citizenship (Chapter 7 by Maaß), social issues (Chapter 6 by Southwell) and corporate social responsibility (Chapter 8 by Graafland *et al.*) are terms employed which convey a concept of positive moral contribution to society but lack any clearer definition. Southwell (Chapter 6) notes that corporate social responsibility is not a very useful perspective to take for SMEs, suggesting a wider approach to responsibility is needed. In this book we have been all-embracing, and while this has resulted in a meaningful collection of papers, we would accept the criticism that we have not furthered the clarification of defining the meaning of social and ethical phrases which have been employed.

The importance of sector

We firmly support the need for sector focus in future SME research. The work by Schmidpeter and Spence (Chapter 4) demonstrates this clearly and it is acknowledged by Southwell in Chapter 6 and Spence and Rutherfoord in Chapter 3. Two of the chapters used specific sector samples. Graafland *et al.* in Chapter 8 focused on construction, metal manufacturing, financial services and wholesale traders. They found that the metal manufacturing and construction sectors were more actively using formal strategies and instruments for organising corporate social responsibility than financial services companies and wholesalers. Schmidpeter and Spence (Chapter 4) interviewed owner-managers from the three sectors of garages, marketing services, and food processing and manufacturing in their sample. In their research, garages were found to be engaged with their immediate community, not only through space negotiation with local neighbours but also as locally orientated businesses. Food processing and manufacturing firms were more likely to be engaged through their employees as larger employers concerned with reputation and recruitment issues. Marketing service organisations were often well networked but not necessarily in relation to their immediate location, being most likely to use new media and inter-regional business networks.

There are commonalities within small firm sectors which need to be addressed more closely. This has major implications for future research and policy recommendations for influencing and supporting SMEs. It is vitally important to bring in trade associations, employer organisations and sector-specific unions when aiming to encourage the social awareness of small firms. Such a study might also extend to investigating suppliers and customers in the sector, and assessing their influence on the behaviour of SMEs. In this way a deeper picture of sector-specific issues can be identified. Furthermore, in some regions a particular sector may have a disproportionate influence on the community due to its presence. This is easily observed where the firm is large and dominates a town or region (such as BASF in Ludwigshafen, Philips in Eindhoven or Boots in Nottingham), but may also occur where many small firms of a similar sector are clustered in a region. For example there is a predominance of the food, hotel and catering sectors in the West London region because of the presence of Heathrow; indeed seven of Janjuha-Jivraj's twelve respondents in her West London research reported on in Chapter 5 belong to these sectors. We support a keener awareness of sectoral distinction in future research on social issues and SMEs.

Regional variations

The regional contexts of study may have an impact on small firm research, although we would not normally expect this to result in greater variations than sector differences. Major regional variations may occur where there is a specific character affecting all local firms, such as the reunification in Germany and the changes which enveloped the ex-German Democratic Republic counties (*Neue Bundesländer*). Regional prosperity or decline may influence the social world of SMEs. It is unclear whether difficult times and circumstances would sharpen competition and encourage ruthless behaviour among SMEs or indeed set an environment in which owner-managers become more involved with colleagues and civic life. The research presented in this volume does not really grapple with this issue and there is room for research on regional variation and sensible application of national policies to influence smaller firms.

National variations

The national contexts in this volume were restricted to Germany, the Netherlands and the United Kingdom. Given the reach of the European Union, there are clear requirements for research that encompasses other European countries and indeed the new members from central and eastern Europe and those which aspire to EU membership. Differing national approaches to engagement will require sensitive handling from a transnational policy perspective.

National differences exist and need better to be understood through comparative work. On the basis of the studies shown here, it seems that legislative, institutional differences are major factors of difference, not necessarily the entrepreneurial character of the SME owner-manager. As a result we see, for example, the readiness of German SME owner-managers to take part in training programmes and apprenticeships (Chapter 4, Schmidpeter and Spence) and the nationally recognisable characteristic of emphasising social dialogue in the Netherlands (Chapter 8, Graafland *et al.*). The wider implications of such differences certainly need more investigation in the light of EU-wide policy initiatives aimed at SMEs in differing national operating contexts.

Beyond the owner-manager

All the empirical research in this book used the response of the owner-manager as the primary source of data. Inevitably the findings are based on self-reporting of the owner-manager taken on trust, although where in-depth interview techniques were used this should ensure a degree of validity in responses. It would be useful to verify the responses of the owner-manager with other parties – in particular, employees, customers, partners, competitors, suppliers, neighbours – in short, at least all those to whom the owner-manager refers in their discussion of social engagement. Indeed, it might be illuminating to gather data from parties with whom the owner-manager is not actively concerned. Triangulation of the data using additional techniques such as participant observation, interview and questionnaire surveys would also enhance reliability and generalisability of the various findings.

Further investigation into the owner-manager as a person, not just his or her role from a business perspective, would augment existing research. Such a small proportion of women owner-managers are included in the studies presented here that we are unable properly to examine gender issues. Level of education, previous experience and training also deserve detailed consideration. Religious affiliation may also be a factor influencing the owner-manager or his or her family and employees. In the research reported on in Chapter 4 by Schmidpeter and Spence, relationships with the Synagogue, Mosque, Church or Temple were part of the discussions although not presented in detail here. In Chapter 5 by Janjuha-Jivraj, Ismaili Muslim and Vanik Hindu communities were drawn upon. No indication of the impact of differing religious perspectives has been elucidated on in this book, but it is certainly worthy of further consideration.

Continuing on the personal perspective of the owner-manager, the role of the family is an important aspect for future study. There is an indication that life-partners of owner-managers, in practice usually wives, act as a relatively time-rich resource and builders of social capital from which the husband's business could benefit. The full appreciation of this perspective requires interviewing of the family members of SME owner-managers. This might help to understand the owner-manager's family role responsibilities, and how the work-life practices are reflected or contradicted in home life. The work–leisure balance may also become an important perspective in determining the owner-manager's time and energy for work-orientated social issues.

From the micro-level of the owner-manager's family life to the macro-level of relationships with local government bodies, non-governmental organisations, business associations and charities, there is a need for further in-depth understanding. Relationships between large firms and SMEs is likely to be particularly interesting given the usual power imbalance and the response by SMEs to collaborate with each other against their larger counterparts. Previous SME research in areas such as networking and trust, not often specifically thought of as 'socially orientated', needs to be included and considered.

The research in this book has been a catalyst for raising the small and medium sized enterprise perspective on social issues to the agenda at business, academic and governmental fora nationally and internationally. It has brought together people interested in the field and provided a sound empirical basis to build upon in the future. The resultant research agenda is important for regional and national policy-makers in the Netherlands, United Kingdom and Germany, but also further afield.

Policy agenda

Policy-makers wishing to influence the social engagement of small and medium sized enterprises should take note of the following findings highlighted by this collection of research.

The regulatory framework in the Netherlands and Germany is similar, in that trade-based individuals are required to have specific qualifications in order to operate and through which sustained membership of the relevant guild or association is normal. This, coupled with the compulsory membership of the Chamber of Commerce, means that SMEs in Germany and the Netherlands are quite well organised before any voluntary, additional membership or networking is entered into. However, over and above these 'requirements' it would be difficult to argue that the German or Dutch small firms were investing more heavily in social capital and responsibility than the UK ones. UK policy-makers might consider increasing institutional requirements of SMEs, although this is likely to be met with resistance by their representatives who reject calls for what is seen as increased bureaucratisation. Indeed, some owner-managers would argue that if they had less bureaucracy to deal with, they would have more time for social engagement. A more fruitful route to take is to raise awareness for the community in general and SMEs in particular, of the possible forms of engagement and potential benefits for the individual and the firm. This might be done through the media and with public statements of support from the government to positively reinforce engagement. Training programmes and advice could help develop a culture of cooperation and involvement. Ironically in Germany and the Netherlands the problem may be that 'engagement' is seen as a regulatory requirement and not something that requires voluntary input.

We believe that the most productive means of change would be to focus on particular sectors. This is something that may have national-specific parameters, for example acknowledging national legal requirements, but is primarily industry rather than nation based. Trade associations with branches or sister organisations in different countries may be able effectively to work together. Such an approach requires close collaboration with trade associations, employer associations and unions.

Policy-makers should be clear that small and medium sized enterprises are in no sense a homogeneous group which can be bracketed together and a blanket policy applied. In addition to sectoral differences, it is argued in Chapter 3 (Spence and Rutherfoord), Chapter 4 (Schmidpeter and Spence) and Chapter 6 (Southwell) that motivation, orientation toward profit and personality type of the owner-manager are also key. Policy makers would do well to respond carefully to the needs of SMEs by informed, contextualised approaches.

Many of the social issues we have spoken about are not readily legislated for. Certainly, SMEs should not be targeted as the only group who have responsibility for civic engagement. Individuals and organisations at the local, regional, national and supranational levels can also set an example. Encouraging and supporting employee volunteering, charitable giving and secondments are all ways in which an atmosphere in support of socially responsible activity can be fostered. Part of this is acknowledging the workplace as a social place in which many differing perspectives and priorities can be accommodated.

It is in this spirit that we conclude this book. If we have encouraged the understanding that responsibility and social capital are part of the social world of the SME, and the research presented begins to reflect what role these concepts play, then the book has been a success.

Appendix: European Commission SME Definitions

Criterion	*Micro*	*Small*	*Medium*
Maximum number of employees	9	49	249
Maximum annual turnover	Not applicable	7 million euros	40 million euros
Maximum annual balance sheet total	Not applicable	5 million euros	27 million euros
Maximum % owned by one or several enterprises not satisfying the same criteria	Not applicable	25%	25%

Index